Finally Secure

Finally Secure

Practical Skills for the **Anxiously Attached** to Find and Keep Love Without Losing Themselves

Maria Vogel, LMFT

Zeitgeist • New York

*This book is dedicated to the healing of
my family's generational trauma.*

*It's also dedicated to my partner—
thanks for our secure attachment.*

This publication contains the opinions and ideas of its author. It is intended to provide helpful and informative material on the subject matter covered. It is sold with the understanding that the author and publisher are not engaged in rendering professional services in the book. If the reader requires personal assistance or advice, a competent professional should be consulted. The author and publisher specifically disclaim any responsibility for any liability, loss, or risk, personal or otherwise, which is incurred as a consequence, directly or indirectly, of the use and application of any of the contents of this book.

Zeitgeist™
An imprint and division of Penguin Random House LLC
1745 Broadway, New York, NY 10019
zeitgeistpublishing.com
penguinrandomhouse.com

Copyright © 2025 by Penguin Random House LLC

Penguin Random House values and supports copyright. Copyright fuels creativity, encourages diverse voices, promotes free speech, and creates a vibrant culture. Thank you for buying an authorized edition of this book and for complying with copyright laws by not reproducing, scanning, or distributing any part of it in any form without permission. You are supporting writers and allowing Penguin Random House to continue to publish books for every reader. Please note that no part of this book may be used or reproduced in any manner for the purpose of training artificial intelligence technologies or systems.

Zeitgeist™ is a trademark of Penguin Random House LLC.

ISBN: 9798217151400
Ebook ISBN: 9798217151011

Printed in the United States of America
1st Printing

Art © by Lukas Kurka/Shutterstock
Book design by Katy Brown
Author photograph © by Bryan Coppede
Edited by Kim Suarez

The authorized representative in the EU for product safety and compliance is Penguin Random House Ireland, Morrison Chambers, 32 Nassau Street, Dublin D02 YH68, Ireland.
https://eu-contact.penguin.ie

Contents

Introduction 6

I: Building Self-Awareness   8

1. Anxiously Attached   10
2. Securely Attached   18

II. Healing Tool Kit for the Anxiously Attached   28

3. Self-Regulation   30
4. Boundaries   46
5. Trust   66
6. Communication   84

III. Being Secure in Love   104

7. Dating and Looking for Love (in All the Wrong Places)   106
8. Relationships and Maintaining Love   124
9. Breakups and Letting Go   143

Conclusion 163
Resources 164
References 166
Index 167
Acknowledgments 174

Introduction

If you're struggling in your relationship with your significant other, or in matters of love in general, I get it. I've been practicing therapy for nine years, and I joke with clients that I had to pay for a graduate-level education to become secure in my own relationships—and now they (and you) get to learn from me! I used to worry I'd be forever stuck in toxic push-pull dynamics. If that's where you are in your journey, let me reassure you that healing is possible, and you deserve healthy, fulfilling relationships.

At the beginning of my career, I worked with foster youth and children with emotional disturbances. I switched to focusing on couples when I realized that children do best when parents or caregivers are well regulated and work together as a team. When families are securely attached, the unit becomes a stable base on which a child can stand.

Even loving parents may have insecurities and unresolved issues that children absorb. Kids are intensely observant, soaking up their environment like a dry sponge. Children's early relationships with caregivers become the blueprint for their relational model, much like a blueprint becomes the foundation for a house. That house starts shaking with anxious attachment when parents display explosive emotions, when their words and actions don't align, or when they dismiss their child's feelings.

People often say, "Nothing that bad happened to me—why do I feel like this?" Even if we don't fully grasp them yet, all our feelings are understandable and make sense. The roots of anxious attachment can take time and a trained eye to see, and that's the goal of this book: to help you understand yourself so you can make new, intentional choices instead of reactive ones.

Maybe you're struggling with dating and finding a relationship that meets your needs. Or maybe you're stuck in a negative cycle with your partner; I know how exhausting and demoralizing it is to be trapped in that fight where no one feels heard, and everyone's frustrated. Sometimes those with anxious attachment have difficulty knowing when to leave a relationship, wondering, *What if I'm leaving something that could be so good, if I tried just a little harder?*

This book will address the top challenges that people with anxious attachment commonly experience in dating, relationships, and love (finding it and letting it go). We'll explore practical tools step by step to help you develop more self-security. Think of building your secure attachment the same way you'd learn to play the guitar—you're not shredding the solo from "Stairway to Heaven" the first time out. Instead, you pluck out "Twinkle, Twinkle, Little Star"—badly. Be patient with yourself as you're learning, and remember that practice leads to improvement. Even small changes are big wins, and those changes will grow over time until you finally feel secure enough in yourself and your relationships.

PART I

Building Self-Awareness

Between stimulus and response there is a space.
In that space is our power to choose our response.
In our response lies our growth and our freedom.

—Viktor Frankl

Awareness is the first step in any healing journey. With increased awareness, we gain the ability to change our behavior when it really matters: in the moment. In this section, you'll start to recognize and name your anxious attachment behaviors so you can make new decisions in tough situations. When we notice our behaviors as they happen, it's much easier to pause, make a different choice, and take one step closer to being secure.

1
Anxiously Attached

Does it feel like you keep dating the same person, just with a different face? You might think, *It's so exciting to meet someone new; this time will be different!* Then, six months in, you're experiencing the same tired problems. Attachment dynamics (not necessarily your partners) may be to blame. This chapter explores different attachment styles, how anxious attachment forms in childhood, what it looks like in adult relationships, and how to move toward security. Awareness of your attachment style is key to changing your patterns. Next time, that new person you like might come with a whole new dynamic, not just a new face.

Attachment Theory

Attachment theory is really all about safety, specifically, the strategies we learned to create safety for ourselves in relationships. *But how can a screaming fight possibly be an attempt to create safety?* you may think. Well, some of us learned to scream our emotions to fight for connection. Others may have learned to avoid conflict altogether by always being agreeable. We might've learned to cling tightly or, conversely, push love away before it can leave.

These behaviors don't make you "bad"—you're just trying to feel safe. The problem is, these actions aren't getting you the desired results of security and connection. Developing secure attachment is about learning to identify your feelings, skillfully ask for what you need, and set appropriate boundaries to take care of yourself. Sometimes it means recognizing when to leave. Think of attachment styles like a partner dance. Anxious people take a step toward their partner, and avoidants take a step back. You're co-creating the dance, but to get in sync, you'll have to learn new moves.

It's the same with attachment behaviors—if you're feeling anxious and call your partner at work for the third time, they might feel stressed and not respond. Their lack of response increases your anxiety, which makes you call again, so they pull away harder by silencing their phone. Who's wrong and who's right in this situation? It's easy to place blame, but maybe you're not trying to hurt each other. You just have different ways of expressing your insecurity. Ultimately, attachment theory explains the different ways people reach out to each other for connection and how they get tripped up.

Attachment Styles

There are two main attachment styles: secure and insecure. All attachment styles exist on a spectrum, and many of us possess elements of both secure and insecure attachment, but we may lean more heavily into insecurity during times of stress or conflict. Our partner makes a difference, too—remember, the dynamic is co-created. Ask yourself which of the following behaviors resonate most with you.

Secure Attachment

This is the goal! Securely attached people trust that a bad moment with their partner is just that: a bad moment. They have enough self-esteem to know that even if they've made a mistake or disappointed their partner, it's not a reflection of themselves as a person. They also have the emotional resilience to tolerate being frustrated or disappointed without blowing up or falling apart. Secure people can communicate clearly and know how to identify and process their emotions so they don't get bottled up and explode. While all of this sounds nice, secure folks aren't perfect and don't have perfect relationships. What they do have is the ability to access positive coping skills, and that allows them to handle the inevitable conflict that arises in relationships.

Insecure Attachment

Insecure attachment is not an official diagnosis like anxiety or depression but a way to understand the strategies and behaviors we use to feel safe in our relationships. Remember that your attachment style isn't fixed, and with positive effort, you can move toward security. While this book's main focus is on anxious attachment, listed next are all of the insecure attachment styles. It's common to have elements of other styles as well. See how each style compares with anxious attachment.

> **Anxious:** Anxiously attached folks spend a lot of time thinking about their relationships. They might mentally write a dissertation about why they didn't get a text back. They tend to obsess over conflict or whether something "feels off" in a relationship. They may appear critical, demanding, or angry when they feel emotionally abandoned or unsupported, but in actuality, they are afraid the person they love most won't be there for them. If they can't get their partner to help them process their feelings, they become desperate for reassurance. So they'll pursue the other person, even if it means causing a fight. To them, fighting is better than no connection at all, and fighting to be heard is better than feeling powerless. Either way, their impulse is to seek out validation from others instead of from within. It's hard for them to tolerate space or disconnect for very long, and trust is usually thin.
>
> **Avoidant:** People with avoidant attachment learned that they might never get their needs met, so why bother trying?

They usually have less preoccupation with relationships and focus more on areas of life where they feel successful, like work or hobbies. In conflict, they resort to logic and reasoning and may become defensive, shut down, or try to convince themselves or others why they shouldn't feel a certain way. They may avoid conflict altogether by saying only what the other person wants to hear (can I get a "Yes, dear"?). Either way, usually, they learned to express upset only internally, not outwardly. Internalized emotions become wrapped in shame, which makes them hard to access. That's why avoidants can seem detached, cold, or uncaring. It's not that they don't feel anything; it's that they can't yet tolerate the shame around their feelings, so they push it all away.

Disorganized: Anxious and avoidant styles are challenging but predictable. Disorganized attachment, however, is unpredictable and confusing—even for the disorganized person! They often share characteristics with both anxious and avoidant types, but they also have a few distinct characteristics that separate them from the other two insecure attachment styles. Many disorganized relationships are "on and off." That might look like terrible verbal (or even physical) fights, followed by periods of relative peace or a "honeymoon" stage. It might look like breaking up and getting back together, or threatening to do so. Disorganized attachment can have a black-and-white quality: One moment your partner is your soulmate; the next you can't stand them. Those with disorganized attachment have difficulty holding two truths: that their partner can care about them but also make mistakes that hurt them. Or that it's OK to have needs, and one person can't meet all of them 100 percent of the time.

The Anxiously Attached

Why are some people securely attached while others are insecure? And what causes some people to be anxious and others avoidant? Let's explore how anxious attachment is created in childhood, how it appears in adult relationships, and how you can use this knowledge to help you move toward more security. The following story illustrates how anxious attachment can begin in childhood and potentially impacts thoughts, behaviors, and beliefs in adult relationships. As you read, please remember that this information is for understanding and awareness, not self-judgment. Be kind to yourself as you make connections to your own life.

Childhood

Jane was 10 when it sank in that her parents might not always be there. It was nobody's fault—one minute, she was laughing with her dad over lunch at a restaurant; the next, he was face-down on the table, caused by too much insulin in his last injection. This wasn't the first time Jane had witnessed her father go into diabetic shock, and she jumped into action, exclaiming, "Call 911!" Miraculously, an off-duty EMT was nearby. He administered oral glucose and called 911, and ultimately, her dad recovered.

Did this situation make Jane's dad a bad parent? Of course not. But the unpredictability of his health due to a lack of self-care created intense and persistent feelings of responsibility and anxiety for Jane, whose core belief grew to be *I have to make sure everyone is safe*.

Anxious attachment develops in homes with chronic unpredictability and/or invalidation. On the surface is a deep desire for connection, but lurking below is a pit of mistrust. If you can't predict your parents' reactions or reliability, it's hard to grow a sense of trust in others. As a baby, you're utterly dependent on adults. The intensity of this need stays with you, so you'll make the relationship work at any cost. Unfortunately, in these situations, that cost is usually the child's self-esteem and security.

Many people with anxious attachment had parents who bottled feelings up and exploded. When an adult unleashes their emotions on a child, a common self-response from kids is *It's my fault*. That's an easier belief to handle than *My parent is out of control*. At least if it's your fault, you can do something different next time, and maybe they won't get so mad.

Adulthood

Jane isn't 10 anymore. She's 27, and now her fear of abandonment is directed at her boyfriend. He's an outdoorsy rock-climbing junkie, and if he hasn't texted by sunset, her mind goes straight to worst-case scenario: *What if he's at the bottom of a ravine with no cell reception?* She blows up his phone, anxiously spiraling until he texts, or she calls his roommates to check if he's home. If he tries to set a boundary, she feels hurt. *Doesn't he care about my anxiety?* Their fights turn into a negative cycle of criticism and defensiveness, tossing blame back and forth like the game hot potato.

In Jane's mind, if her boyfriend understands how much she's hurting, he'll change his behavior, and everything will be OK. It's *his* behavior that's the problem! She thinks she's being vulnerable by sharing her feelings, but her communication methods are ineffective and contribute to the negative cycle. They're co-creating the merry-go-round from hell—an anxious-avoidant dynamic.

Given her experiences with her father, Jane's anxiety is understandable. As an adult, however, she's reacting to childhood triggers by trying to control her partner. Instead of self-soothing, she's demanding that he comfort her. Instead of trusting him to call, she's suspicious and accuses him of not caring about her feelings. Instead of taking responsibility for her well-being, she blames her emotions on his behavior.

While her boyfriend's avoidance is a problem, healing anxious attachment in adult relationships requires taking radical accountability for oneself.

2
Securely Attached

If you're living with anxious attachment, the previous story may feel painfully familiar. But how is a securely attached relationship supposed to feel? I've found that most anxious people truly don't know, despite their strong desire to experience it. Moving from anxiety to security starts with self-soothing by seeking internal validation rather than external—a vital first step to avoid building a relationship with the wrong person or sabotaging a relationship with the right one. If you're overly focused on external validation, it's much harder to develop self-trust. Let's explore secure attachment and how to build it in your adult life.

Secure Attachment

What would've helped Jane develop into a securely attached adult? No parent is perfect, and there are circumstances that are out of even the most attentive parent's control—like a chronic illness. Does that mean we're all doomed to insecure attachment? Thankfully not! In this section, we'll explore how secure attachment forms. This will help you begin to see what might have been incomplete or missing in your childhood experiences.

Building Blocks

After the incident in the restaurant, Jane told her dad she was afraid of him dying. His response stemmed from his own insecurities: "Don't say that, Janie! That makes me sad. I'm fine." Not the worst reaction, but it lacked *attunement*, in this case, by failing to validate Jane's emotions or reflect her experience.

Secure parents attune by validating their child's emotions, teaching the child that their internal experience can be trusted and reflects reality on some level. True emotional attunement comes from validation that's offered with empathy. It's the difference between saying "I understand" and showing that you truly understand with your tone, facial expression, and body language. Attunement allows the child to feel seen, heard, and understood. Without some degree of attunement, an anxious child's feelings escalate in an attempt to be heard and avoid emotional abandonment. In Jane's case, she was left feeling guilty for making her dad feel bad. She internalized the message *We can't talk about this; my feelings are too much for him.*

All parents make mistakes, but securely attached parents repair them afterward. Unfortunately, Jane's father missed the mark and let his own anxiety get in the way of being present for hers. A secure response might have been, "It must have been so scary to see me faint and be afraid of losing me. I'm sorry. I'm here," or "This wasn't your fault. It's my job to take care of myself, not yours."

Ideally, secure attachment is formed in childhood. But not everyone is so lucky. However, if you're a person with an anxious attachment style, it's absolutely possible to build security now by reparenting yourself in ways you needed as a child but didn't receive. That means catching yourself in the moment of a trigger, giving yourself what your parent or guardian didn't know that you needed at the time, and making a healthier choice. Validating yourself takes practice if it wasn't modeled for you. It isn't easy, but it's worth the effort.

Adult Relationships

Adult relationships also need attunement and repair to build security. If Jane were more securely attached, would she be "cool" with her boyfriend's lack of communication? Doubtful. Secure folks still have needs. The difference is, they have stronger self-regulation skills, which allows them to express feelings with vulnerability instead of blame.

Secure regulation skills come from the ability to recognize, understand, and label one's own emotions. For example, a more secure Jane would notice that she was ruminating and take a pause. If she didn't know why she felt irritable, she could self-reflect and come to a deeper understanding: *I'm anxious because my boyfriend hasn't called to check in. That's understandable, considering my dad's history of health scares.*

Timing also matters. Jane could have waited to express herself until her boyfriend was home and well rested. Instead of popping off, she could have gone to the gym or called a friend to process. Secure folks can differentiate between feelings of urgency and an actual emergency, so they're less reactive.

Secure people don't typically fall into their own interpretation of what's happening—they communicate their fears vulnerably. Vulnerability in this context is the ability to communicate feelings without blaming. It may sound like "I want you to have fun rock climbing. At the same time, I feel anxious when you've been gone for hours without calling. I worry about your safety, like I did with my dad. Can we find a solution that meets both our needs?"

Vulnerability reflects emotional maturity; it's a strength, not a weakness. It's also crucial for secure attachment. We'll dive deeper into vulnerability later.

Preparing to Be Truly Secure

Let's face it, relationships are not for wimps! Learning to be secure takes courage, willingness, and patience with mistakes. If you're prepared to do the work, though, the payoff is amazing, benefiting both you and your relationships. Healthy relationships can be a wonderful source of support, companionship, and fulfillment. More importantly, a secure you means a healthier relationship with *yourself*, and that's the real win.

Make the commitment now to always remind yourself that it takes hard work to make real and lasting change. As you embark on your journey toward secure attachment, consider the following tips to help you stay the course when you encounter obstacles and self-limiting beliefs.

Actionable Tip 1: Take Radical Accountability

Remember how Jane blamed her boyfriend for not texting quickly enough? Hard truth: Anxiously attached people can struggle to take accountability for their own part in relationships. Blame feels safe, so it's easy to blame the other person (in this case, Captain Avoidant over there). *If they could just change, I wouldn't have to feel this way. It's them; their behavior is the problem!*

OK, you're right, Jane—Captain Avoidant is contributing to the problem. And, said with tough love, so are you. You can control only one of these people, and it's not your partner. I encourage you to shift your focus back to yourself and ask, *What can I do more skillfully?*

This is *radical accountability*. While it might seem unfair at first, it's actually empowering. Finding the most honest and skillful way to communicate feelings is the real *Art of War*: "The greatest victory is that which requires no battle." This is good advice for war *and* relationships! Instead of battling your partner to change, claim victory by changing yourself.

The best reason for radical accountability is that it's the only way to know whether the relationship is viable. When Jane acted out by repeatedly calling her boyfriend, she always felt guilty and ashamed afterward. She worried, *Am I overreacting? Am I ruining something good?* This questioning kept her stuck, waffling between doubting herself and doubting the relationship. Only when Jane changed *her* behavior could she evaluate with a clearer head.

Through the process of radical accountability, you'll know when it's time to leave a relationship: when you've truly changed but the relationship hasn't.

Actionable Tip 2: Be Patient

Urgency is a common feeling with anxious attachment. A young child's needs really are urgent. When a baby needs food, their cries demand that their needs be met *now*. The adult version of this looks like needing to talk to your partner *now* or needing to resolve an issue *immediately*. If you can't, you'll soon be swirling in anxiety or frustration.

Jane felt panicked when she didn't hear from her boyfriend after rock climbing. To manage her anxiety, she demanded to hear from him as soon as he got cell service back. Jane's childhood situation with her father involved actual emergencies, so she brought that same sense of urgency to her relationship, even when it wasn't called for.

Patience means slowing down and differentiating between that actual emergency and your internal feeling of urgency. Both situations activate your body's survival energy: fight, flight, freeze, or fawn (people-pleasing). If you're feeling one of those responses in your body, ask yourself, *Is anyone physically hurt or in danger? If I pause to calm down, is anything bad certain to happen?* If the answer is no, you're feeling urgency in a non-emergency, so go ahead and calm your body down before taking action. Trust that whatever the problem, it'll be resolved eventually.

Patience also means offering kindness and respect to yourself when you make mistakes. Growth isn't always linear—sometimes the path up a mountain goes downhill, but you're still climbing. Security is truly a skill you can learn with practice, so trust the process and lead with a mindset of progress over perfection.

Actionable Tip 3: Take the Lead

You may ask yourself, *Shouldn't my partner take accountability, too?* Ideally, you're both accountable. Sometimes, however, you have to take the lead to effect the change you want. Rather than seeing this situation as unfair, look at it as a chance to be the leader in your own life.

If your partner doesn't validate you, instead of correcting them, embody change by modeling how you want to be spoken to—with respect. Committing to speaking respectfully, no matter what, improves emotional safety by decreasing hurtful words, and that inspires change. It works better than saying "You're doing it wrong again."

Jane chose not to call her boyfriend after his last rock-climbing adventure. Instead, she went on a friend date and then to the gym. She gave her partner all the space in the world—and he still didn't check in! When she brought it up the next day, he got defensive: "I told you, I'm exhausted after rock climbing! I don't call because I'm hungry and tired. It's not about you."

Undeterred, Jane took the lead by modeling her new communication skills: "I've been critical about this in the past, so I understand why you're defending yourself. This isn't all your fault. I want to feel safe, and I want you to feel free. How can we do this together?"

Does taking the lead guarantee the other person will respond the way you want? Sadly, no. However, continuously leading makes it more likely they will respond favorably and eventually follow suit. Conversely, this approach can also shed light on a relationship that's unlikely to be fixed. If the other person can't respond in kind to your repeated efforts to communicate with vulnerability, you'll know soon enough.

Actionable Tip 4:
Build Your Relationship with Yourself

All these relationship skills don't apply just to your relationship with a partner. You can also use them with the most important person in your life: you!

Many clients ask, "What's wrong with me? Why am I such a mess?" I always respond, "Would you say that to your best friend? No? Then why is it OK to say to yourself?"

Unfortunately, most of us were taught—either implicitly or explicitly—to relate to ourselves through criticism and shame. Many people think, *If I'm not hard on myself, how will I grow as a person?* Instead, ask yourself, *Has being hard on myself really upgraded my quality of life and relationships?* If not, then give yourself grace and try something new. We all deserve kindness. Security blossoms when we foster a better relationship with ourselves just as we would with others—through validation, respect, and healthy boundaries.

Like any relationship, the one with yourself requires maintenance and will have ups and downs. You can improve it significantly by validating your own feelings and being kind to yourself when you're struggling, just like you would with a friend. Self-validating means acknowledging that your feelings are understandable.

Jane started practicing self-validation as the first step toward soothing her anxiety: *I'm scared and desperate to hear from him. My anxiety is real, and this isn't an emergency; it's just a hard moment. I'm not going to abandon myself to chase after him. I'm going to move my body to process this anxious energy.*

Validating yourself confirms that you're worthy of respect, which builds self-security. It's a lifelong job, but the more you practice, the more naturally it will come to you. Looking back, you'll be so proud of how far you've come.

PART II

Healing Tool Kit for the Anxiously Attached

Now that we've explored what attachment is and how it forms during childhood, let's dive into the skill-building tools to reach your goal of secure attachment. While it's easy to feel stuck, you *can* change your attachment style. In this part of the book, we'll explore four main skill categories that anxiously attached people need to develop to become secure: self-regulation, boundaries, trust, and communication.

In each chapter, we'll identify the tools, step by step, to help you learn each new skill. These skills don't come overnight, but by practicing, you'll be better equipped and more confident in knowing how to handle dating, relationships, and even breakups.

3
Self-Regulation

Self-regulation is more than just calming down or being "chill." It's about identifying feelings and learning to ride waves of emotion as they peak and fall. Secure people have feelings, same as the rest of us; they're just more skilled at handling difficult moments without shutting down or falling apart. Anxiously attached people often want co-regulation, or to have someone else help them calm down. While this desire is natural and necessary as a child, as adults we become responsible for our emotional states, so let's go over some coping skills. Try them for the first time when you're feeling relaxed, rather than in the thick of panic.

Tool 1
Trigger Map

YOU WILL LEARN
- Your personal triggers
- Your body's signals

YOU WILL NEED
- 30 minutes to yourself
- Writing tools

Everyone has emotional triggers, or specific situations and subjects that they react to. All emotions are tied to physical sensations, such as our heart racing when we're scared. The nervous system can't differentiate between emotional and physical stress, so our body reacts the same way to a robbery as it does to our partner being angry. That's why our reactions can feel so big. Do you know what triggers you? Can you tell when you're triggered? Awareness of your body's signals is the first step toward self-regulation. Let's build a map to help you understand your triggers and their signals.

Picture this: You come home from a long day at work. Your partner's sitting at their desk. The sink is full of last night's dishes, and your overflowing trash can looks like Oscar the Grouch's penthouse.

Nobody would be happy to walk in on this scene. However, you can choose how to react, and that choice may determine how the rest of the night unfolds. Slow things down by identifying your body signals and exploring the reasoning behind them.

1. **Identify your body signals.** Body signals are the most immediate sign that you're experiencing emotions. That tight chest

and racing heart are literally your body alerting you: *Something's wrong.* By listening to those signals, you can create space around your reaction, like breathing, before you respond.

2. **Connect signals with emotions.** You're tired after a long day, and this is not what you wanted to deal with. A surge of adrenaline hints that a fight is coming on. Your racing heart is telling you, *I'm upset*. Noticing your body's signals and labeling your feelings helps you pause, self-soothe, and express yourself thoughtfully.

3. **Consider the deeper meaning.** We're not usually that mad about what transpired—we're upset by the meaning we've created. The real upset is probably not the dishes themselves; rather, it's the deeper meaning of *you value your time over mine*. While these feelings are understandable, they're rocket fuel for conflict and don't leave room for mutual understanding.

4. **Investigate the trigger.** The final column helps you make connections to core beliefs that are coloring your feelings. We form these beliefs in childhood, and they become the lens through which we see the world. When our partner doesn't hear us, it feels like evidence that our core belief is true—*we must not be worthy of being heard*. The core belief is what we're usually really fighting against. When we understand what's actually triggering us, it's easier to separate from the past, challenge our distorted beliefs, and respond to the present moment more objectively.

Think of recent times you felt upset about a relational problem, and complete the table to build a "map" of your inner world. Look for themes around what triggers you and how your body responds.

What happened? *Example: Chores didn't get done*

_____

What were my body signals? *Example: Tightness in my chest, clenching my fists*

_____

_____

How did I feel? *Example: Frustrated, annoyed, defeated, angry*

_____

_____

What's the deeper meaning? *Example: Feeling unimportant, unheard, like my requests don't matter*

_____

_____

Why was this so triggering? *Example: I felt unheard in my family. If my requests aren't heard, it means I'm not worthy.*

_____

_____

Tool 2
Self-Validation

YOU WILL LEARN
- Why self-validation is important
- Examples of self-validation
- How to validate yourself

YOU WILL NEED
- 15 minutes to yourself
- Writing tools

A like on a selfie, a compliment—who doesn't love a little external validation? Despite this, one of the most important skills for anxiously attached people to develop is *self*-validation. With anxious attachment, the tendency is to pursue recognition from others, which almost never ends well. It's too much pressure to put on a partner, and it usually pushes the other person away. Self-validation is really about self-respect and saying, *I'm worthy of kindness*. Let's explore how to handle things the next time you need to validate your own feelings.

Say you're hoping for a text from last night's date. It was a great time, hopping from a bar to dinner to a comedy show. As you said good night, your date asked you to text them when you got home. So, you texted, "Home safe, thanks for a lovely evening! Let's do it again soon."

Twenty-four hours later, nothing. Instead of texting your friends a screenshot captioned "What does it MEAN?" try these steps:

1. Identify a specific body signal (racing heart, tension, ruminating thoughts, etc.).

2. Identify your feelings (anxious, disappointed, hurt, etc.).

3. Validate your emotions with kindness (examples to follow).

This three-step strategy is all about mindfulness. More than just meditation or having an "empty mind," mindfulness is about noticing our thoughts, feelings, and behaviors, with the magical added ingredient: kindness. See, most of us notice our feelings with shame and judgment, but that doesn't create sustainable change. The kinder you are to yourself, the more success you'll have in calming down. Try phrases like these:

- *I was looking forward to another date. I'm allowed to be disappointed.*

- *I'm nervous I won't hear back. That makes sense.*

- *Uncertainty is hard. It's OK that I'm still learning to manage the unknown.*

- *Even if I don't hear back, I'll be OK. It'll hurt, but putting myself out there is brave.*

- *I'm anxious to hear back, but it hasn't been that long yet. I don't know what the other person is thinking.*

- *It's stressful not to know why I haven't heard back. I don't have to assume the worst.*

Try offering yourself some self-validation here, using a recent experience in your own words:

_____

_____

_____

Make self-validation a habit! Start applying self-validation to your own life, even in small ways. The more you practice, the easier and more natural it will become.

Tool 3
Breathing Exercises

YOU WILL LEARN
- Why breathing works for self-regulation
- How to breathe mindfully
- Practical applications

YOU WILL NEED
- 15 minutes to yourself
- A safe place to practice

Breathing is the physiological function we can control most easily. Slower breathing forces your heart rate to slow down, decreasing your blood pressure and calming your body. I've had clients say, "I'm annoyed this works so well." Breathing exercises are effective because they work *with* your body, de-escalating the cascade of stress hormones flooding your system. Many times, anxiously attached folks want to fight their anxiety, but that just makes the feelings bigger. Breathing leans in and shows you *it's OK; we'll get through this*.

You don't need to solve any problems yet—for now, you're just reminding your body that this isn't an emergency. First calm down, and then figure out the next step.

Learning to self-regulate, like any skill, requires practice. But the time to learn new breathing exercises isn't in the middle of a panic attack. You'll do better if you practice these exercises the first few times when you're calm and in a safe place. That way, they're familiar when you need them.

Set a timer for at least two minutes—that's the minimum amount of time breathing takes to be effective. You'll need longer if you're very stressed, so keep going until you feel calmer. Try them all, and see which exercise is your favorite.

Exercise 1: 4-6-8 Breathe

Breathe in for a count of four.

Hold your breath for a count of six.

Breathe out for a count of eight.

The most popular breathing exercise among my clients, this one works because holding your breath forces your heart rate to slow down.

Exercise 2: Breathe with this GIF

Search for the phrase "breathe with this GIF." A thousand moving images should pop up, including cute cats and LeBron James. Choose your favorite, and save it on your phone in a special album for anxiety. Breathe with the moving image. Most are set for four seconds of inhaling and eight seconds of exhaling. Clear your mind and breathe along.

Exercise 3: Box Breathing

Draw a box with a pencil or trace one with your finger as you breathe. Start drawing horizontally while inhaling for four seconds. Then draw vertically down while holding your breath for four seconds. Exhale for four seconds as you draw across the bottom. Hold your breath for four seconds as you draw back up. Repeat the process at least four more times or until you feel calmer. Use the diagram as an example.

The best part about breathing exercises: No one can tell you're doing them! Everyone is breathing all the time, so no one's going to notice if you're breathing intentionally. You can also combine breathing exercises with other self-regulation tools, like Self-Validation (Tool 2, page 34).

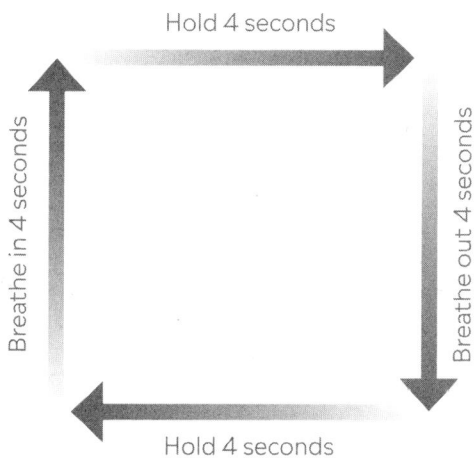

Tool 4
Sensory Soothing

YOU WILL LEARN
- How to get in touch with your senses
- Multiple forms of sensory soothing

YOU WILL NEED
- 15 minutes to yourself
- A safe place to practice
- Something cold
- Something strongly flavored

When we're upset, it's easy to become overstimulated and overwhelmed. Thankfully, we can use our senses to come back to our center. Ever heard of multitasking? Yeah, it doesn't exist (at least not in the brain's ability to process sensory input). The human brain genuinely can't process multiple streams of information at once. You can use that to your advantage by focusing on one sense at a time to calm down in a stressful moment. This tool will provide space between stimulus and response. These exercises are especially helpful for intense emotions that come on suddenly, like panic or anger.

You just got an ambiguous text from the person you're dating: "Hey, can we talk today?" Your mind is splitting into a multiverse of possibilities.

Now's the time to
- Notice body signals
- Self-regulate

Now's not the time to
- Text back
- Try to guess what they're thinking
- Take action

Try all of these exercises and see which one resonates most with you.

Exercise 1: Hold the Cold

Grab something cold—an ice cube, frozen fruit, or an ice pack. Sit comfortably and hold the cold for at least five minutes. You can also add a breathing exercise (Tool 3, page 37).

You don't have to solve anything; just focus on the sensation of coldness. Hold it in your hands or against your arms, face, legs, or other body part. If your mind wanders into story or fix-it mode, bring your attention back to the cold. It might help to visualize standing in a snowy field or imagine you're a baby seal on an iceberg. Keep holding the cold for at least five minutes.

If you can't stand cold, try heat instead. Microwave a damp towel or water bottle, or run a very warm bath, and follow the same instructions.

Exercise 2: Hum

Humming is a great way to focus your mind and simmer down. The vibration gives strong sensory input and stimulates the vagus nerve, a key part of the parasympathetic nervous system that calms and restores the body.

Combine humming with deep breathing. Inhale for a count of four. On the exhale, start humming and continue for a count of eight. If helpful, cover your ears. Repeat the cycle for at least two minutes.

Exercise 3: Pucker Up

This exercise is the fastest-acting sensory remedy. If you're feeling a strong emotion, engage your sense of taste—you'll find that it's hard to focus on anything else. Strong flavors include spicy, minty, or sour. Try Altoids mints or Warheads or Sour Patch Kids candies; just choose something you can enjoy or at least tolerate. Afterward, if you're still feeling anxious, try another sensory-soothing tool.

In all of these exercises, if your mind drifts, keep drawing your focus back to your senses; your thoughts will settle down, and your feelings will float to the surface. Tears might come to relieve the tension. Crying is healthy and releases endorphins that help us feel better. Allow yourself to feel whatever you need.

Tool 5
Move Your Body

YOU WILL LEARN
- Why exercise helps you self-regulate
- Specific exercises for self-regulation

YOU WILL NEED
- 30 minutes to yourself
- Space to do basic movement
- A yoga mat or towel

In the nervous system, emotions rise, peak, and fall. We often build a dam against their flow, meaning pressure builds over time before bursting from the tiniest drop of distress. It's usually better for us (and our relationships) if we notice our body signals in the moment, feel the energy rise, and release it skillfully. Exercise is one of the healthiest ways to do that because it helps emotions move through the nervous system naturally.

But I hate exercise. I have no discipline! If this sounds like you, ask yourself, *Do I really hate all exercise, or do I hate the exercises I'm forcing myself to do?* For daily or weekly exercise, choose something you actually enjoy. Is it dance, roller-skating, sports? Moving your body is easier when you're doing it for fun.

If discipline is a concern, try *behavioral activation*—a fancy phrase for just starting the exercise, setting a timer for 7 to 10 minutes, and seeing how you feel when the timer goes off. We want motivation to fall from heaven, but sadly, that's not how motivation works. Instead, we have to start the behavior; the motivation to finish gets activated while we're doing it. Annoying but true.

Try setting timers for these exercises, and see if it helps your motivation and consistency.

Exercise 1: Go for a Walk

Basic, but it gets the job done. A walk in nature or around the block for at least 20 or 30 minutes every day is very effective, especially if you're feeling stirred up. Listen to music or a podcast to take your mind off any worries. Break up the walk into 10-minute increments if you can't spare more time in one go.

Exercise 2: Hold Plank Pose

If you're feeling anxious, stressed, or frustrated, try holding plank pose for increments of 30 seconds, or as long as you can, for a total of two minutes. Adjust for your physical ability. Ideally, you'll tremor a little toward the end of the pose. This works with your body's natural stress reliever: shaking! Shaking tells your body to relieve stress. Holding a plank also has the added benefit of strengthening your core. Who knew anxiety gave you abs of steel?

Exercise 3: Shake It Off

Get an anxiety-provoking message from someone? Shake it off! Stand up and shimmy your legs, shake your arms, and flap your hands like your body is in an earthquake. Or imagine a Chihuahua at the vet, and embody that vibe. Set a timer for two minutes, taking breaks as needed. This is another way to induce shaking.

When we work with our body's natural systems for stress relief, our emotions become more manageable. This helps us feel more capable and self-confident. Over time, this is how we build self-trust and self-esteem.

4

Boundaries

Healthy boundaries are one of the best ways for anxiously attached people to feel closer in their relationships. *But wait! Don't boundaries divide us?* Actually, boundaries reflect our needs, show others how to treat us, and help us develop an internal sense of security. Holding boundaries cultivates self-trust. When you trust your ability to honor your needs and boundaries appropriately, your self-esteem will improve, and your relationships will feel less pressured and resentful. By setting clear boundaries with your partner, you create predictability and a more secure attachment environment, which makes everyone feel safer—and that's the goal!

Tool 6
Boundaries Versus Requests

YOU WILL LEARN
- The difference between boundaries and requests
- How to identify your boundaries
- How to express boundaries skillfully

YOU WILL NEED
- 30 minutes to yourself
- Awareness of things that bother you
- Writing tools

Boundaries are necessary for secure attachment. People commonly say, "I set boundaries all the time. They just aren't respected!" If you're feeling run over, make sure you're communicating boundaries and not requests. It's easy to confuse the two. Boundaries are about you—how *you* will respond if your boundaries are crossed. Requests are what we ask of others, and they may or may not follow through. Let's explore how to effectively reframe requests as boundaries.

Imagine this: Your partner borrowed your car last night. This morning, you open your car door and are greeted by squished mayo packets, greasy wrappers, the lingering waft of stale fries—and not for the first time! Staying silent builds resentment. So you say, "Stop eating fast food in my car! It's messy and smells for days!"

I get it—nobody wants a McNuggets air freshener, and everyone wants to feel heard and respected. However, this is a request, and requests put the responsibility on the other person, who may not comply. Boundaries acknowledge the other person, state our needs, and explain what will happen if our boundary is crossed again. Here's an example: "I understand you get hungry while driving. At the same time, having my space respected is important to me. My car won't be available to borrow if you continue eating in it."

There's the difference. Requests ("Stop eating in my car") ask the other person to do something, and boundaries ("If you can't respect my car, I will not let you use it") are about *you* and what you will do if someone crosses your line. They require the other person to do *nothing*.

Think of boundaries you want in your own relationships, and record them in the following chart. It can help to imagine a behavior you dislike, then think about what you need instead. Make sure to communicate with vulnerability rather than blame, and use empathy while staying true to yourself. The example provided in the chart shows how you can be both vulnerable ("I want to be respected") and empathetic ("I want you to be respected, too").

Finally, you don't always have to explain that you're setting a boundary; simply enforce it with your behavior, like not lending your car. This would be your nonverbal response. Think of a behavior you dislike and fill in the table on the next page by following the examples.

Remember, don't expect others to celebrate your boundaries. Just hold them—they're for you, not anyone else. It's easier with practice, and your future self will feel proud and so empowered.

Behavior I dislike
Example: Yelling

_____

_____

What is my need?
Example: To feel respected during fights

_____

_____

Boundary
Example: I want us both to feel respected. If we start yelling, I'll excuse myself to calm down. I'll be back in an hour to talk again.

_____

_____

Nonverbal response
Example: Create a signal that you're overwhelmed, then leave.

_____

_____

Tool 7
Identify and Express Your Needs

YOU WILL LEARN
- How to identify your needs
- How to set boundaries around needs
- How to express your needs through vulnerability

YOU WILL NEED
- 30 minutes to yourself
- Writing tools

Clients often say, "But if I tell my partner what I need, it won't feel special when I get it." You know what's really special? Getting your needs met. When a partner meets our attachment needs, it provides emotional safety, one of the foundational pieces of secure relationships. It's our job to know and communicate our needs—never the other person's responsibility to guess. Let's explore how to make connections between your childhood experiences and your attachment needs. From there, you can determine how to express your needs in healthy and vulnerable ways.

Who could really love me like this? Underneath all the frustration and people-pleasing, anxiously attached people often struggle with feeling truly lovable. They worry they're too much—too needy, too emotional, too hard to handle.

I promise, you're not too needy. What's usually going on is difficulty communicating the real, deeper need. Most people get stuck in the details of a disagreement, and they never get to the real issue: unmet attachment needs. Don't worry, there's hope!

How did your parents respond to your emotions? Were you sent to your room to deal with it alone? Were you told to "get over it" or "stop making such a big deal"? These are just examples. Apply this exploration to your own experiences.

Even loving parents sometimes resort to unhelpful parenting strategies. If you experienced this kind of parenting, even occasionally, you may have unmet attachment needs. You'll demand those needs be met by your partner, which rarely gets results. A better strategy is to verbally ask for your needs to be met and set boundaries where needed.

To gain clarity around your needs, use the examples to fill in the statements on the next page as they relate to you.

Next, let's think about how to use vulnerability to get your needs met. (See page 91 for more on using assertive vulnerability to share your feelings.) Here's how you might express a need to another person through vulnerability:

"To feel good in this relationship, I need to feel like my concerns matter. Yours matter, too. Can we work on this together?"

And here's one way you can set a boundary around your needs:

"I need to feel understood and heard during conflict. It helps me feel safe. If we can't hear each other right now, I'll take space and come back when we're calmer."

In my childhood, my emotions were . . .
Example: Minimized, dismissed, met with an explosion

_____

In my childhood, I often felt . . .
Example: Lonely, tossed aside, blamed

_____

In my relationships, I've felt . . .
Example: Unheard, unimportant, ignored

_____

I want to feel . . .
Example: Understood, validated, prioritized

_____

_____

If my needs are met, I will feel . . .
Example: Fulfilled, cherished, safe, loved, important

_____

_____

Tool 8
Respecting Others' Boundaries

YOU WILL LEARN
- How to respect others' boundaries
- What to do when you want to pursue

YOU WILL NEED
- 20 minutes to yourself
- Writing tools

Anxious people are most afraid of emotional abandonment, but they accidentally abandon themselves when they pursue! They aren't intentionally crossing boundaries; they're just so desperate to feel heard and connected that they'll resort to almost anything. This often leaves the other person feeling pressured, overwhelmed, and like they can't get anything right. Tough love: Don't abandon yourself to chase after someone else. Instead, listen to your body signals, and respond to them with kind self-soothing. This is how you can reparent yourself and build security.

Let's say you've been dating someone for two months. It's going well, and you've agreed to be exclusive. Everything feels great—except your partner hasn't introduced you to any of their friends. They have a standing game night every Friday, and you're never invited. You've asked to join, but your partner responds with "I move slow. I'm not ready to introduce you to my friends yet."

You have a few options.

You could pursue:
- Ask, "Why not? If this relationship is important to you, you'll introduce me!"
- Demand a date night on Fridays.
- Text on Fridays telling them how hurt you are.

Or you can pause:
- Accept the boundary and notice how it makes you feel. It's OK to feel disappointed, sad, or left out.
- Observe your body signals.
- Use a self-soothing tool (Tool 4, page 40) if you're too upset to respond calmly.

Once you've regulated, you can state your needs while acknowledging the other person. "I respect that you're being intentional about introducing me to your friends. It's wise to take things slow. At some point, it'll be important for me to meet them. I'm looking for a relationship where we're integrated in each other's lives in a healthy way. How do you feel about that?"

From here, plan out your Friday nights so you're not obsessing over game night. Make your own plans with friends, go to a concert, or hit the gym. Engage with yourself instead of banging on a closed door. You'll feel less frustrated, and your partner will have the space they need to feel safe, especially if your partner shows signs of having an avoidant attachment style. When an avoidant partner feels safe, they're more likely to give you the connection you want. Then it's a win-win!

In the meantime, take some time to write out body signals that come up when you want to pursue and what you can do to self-soothe.

Then jot down ways you can turn toward yourself instead of focusing on the other person.

Body signals that tell me I'm feeling insecure and want to pursue:

_____

_____

Ways I can self-soothe (for ideas, revisit Breathing Exercises, page 37; Sensory Soothing, page 40; and Move Your Body, page 43):

_____

_____

Ways I can focus on myself:

_____

_____

_____

Tool 9
Reasonable Expectations

YOU WILL LEARN
- Unreasonable versus reasonable expectations
- How to manage expectations

YOU WILL NEED
- 30 minutes to yourself
- Writing tools

"It's not fair. I would do *anything* for them!" This is a common complaint I hear, but the fact is we shouldn't be willing to do *anything* for anyone. It's healthy to have limits. Sometimes we're upset because we gave a lot to someone but they aren't willing to do the same. Take stock of how often you cross your own boundaries to stay in connection with someone else. This act of taking stock is radical accountability.

If you're feeling frustrated that you've given more in your relationships than your partners have, ask yourself, *Are my expectations reasonable?* This applies to your expectations of yourself *and* others.

Let's create a table to explore healthy and unhealthy expectations. How can we reframe the unhealthy ones?

Look at the following examples. Think about your own experiences, and apply the same exploration by filling in the boxes. Be honest with yourself!

Unhealthy expectations of myself
Examples: To never make mistakes / To always be happy / To always give to others

___

Healthy expectations of myself
Examples: To try my best / To be kind / To maintain and respect boundaries

___

Unhealthy relationship expectations
Examples: One person should meet all my needs. / Others should be there for me immediately. / Others should calm me down.

___

Healthy relationship expectations
Examples: To be empathetic and validating / To be honest with each other / To discuss conflict respectfully

___

Reframes for unhealthy expectations
Examples: Everyone makes mistakes. \ No one can give me everything all the time. \ Emotions fluctuate, like everything.

___

What if I can't tell whether my expectations are unreasonable? A helpful tip is to ask yourself if there's an implied "should" in your expectation. They *should* know what I need. They *should* meet all my needs. Don't should on yourself, friend!

Our expectations are tied to our beliefs about ourselves and the world. So, another way to vet your expectations is to ask yourself, *What does it mean if my partner can't meet all my needs? Does it mean they're selfish and uncaring? Does it mean I'm too much?* If an expectation leads to a negative belief about yourself or others, it's probably unreasonable. Find a more flexible (and accurate) reframe: *No one can meet anyone's needs 100 percent of the time, and that's why we have friends and community in addition to our partners.*

Despite what you've seen on Instagram, no relationship is perfect. Instead of aiming for perfection, try for "good enough." A good-enough relationship should feel positive most of the time, with occasional bumps that are repaired successfully. Conflict happens—it's inevitable, and even necessary. But reasonable expectations allow partners to enjoy a healthier balance of you, me, and us.

Tool 10
Understanding Guilt

YOU WILL LEARN
- Guilt versus toxic guilt
- How to work through toxic guilt

YOU WILL NEED
- 30 minutes to yourself
- Knowledge of your values
- Writing tools

Guilt has a bad reputation, but it has a purpose. When we act out of alignment with our values, guilt is there to remind us to get back in line. There's a second kind of guilt, though, that's less productive. If you feel like "the worst" for enforcing a boundary, such as saying no, you may be experiencing toxic guilt. Boundaries can feel scary when you're used to people-pleasing or aren't in touch with your own needs. This is normal—you'll get more confident with your boundaries with practice. Let's explore how to set boundaries *and* minimize toxic guilt.

No one is going to die if you say no. Still, I understand the sentiment. Fill out the following worksheet, and let's talk about how to take care of yourself through the process.

1. Imagine your best friend. What would you say if someone kept asking them for money? Would you tell them to keep giving, or would you encourage them to speak up for themselves? Now, follow your own advice! Write a message to yourself as you

would to a friend, encouraging yourself to set a boundary in a needed area.

_____

_____

_____

2. Would you be upset if someone set a boundary with you? If the answer is no, then shouldn't you be allowed to do the same? Think about a boundary someone has set with you in the past. How did it make you feel?

_____

_____

_____

3. Remember your "why." Are you setting boundaries because you *want* to hurt the other person? Probably not. Boundaries are about owning our values, such as honesty, self-respect, integrity, and compassion. It's possible to set boundaries that include all of these and more. Set boundaries because you respect the other person (and yourself) enough to be honest with them. Write out the values you want to embody as you set boundaries.

_____

_____

_____

4. Think of flexible reframes and repeat them to yourself when you're feeling toxic guilt creep up on you. Read these examples, and then write down your own!

- *Feeling guilty doesn't mean I did anything wrong.*
- *I'm not responsible for others' reactions or emotions.*
- *Boundaries aren't selfish.*
- *I feel bad for setting this boundary right now, but no feeling lasts forever.*

_____

_____

_____

Boundaries don't have to be barbed-wire fences. People confuse boundaries with harshness, but they can be simple and gentle while still being firmly held. Imagine a soft glow around you that radiates, *We both deserve respect.* Empathize with the other person, acknowledging them while staying true to yourself. "I know you were looking forward to dancing this weekend, and I'm sorry to cancel. I overbooked myself and need to rest. Can we reschedule for later this month?"

Tool 11
Handling Pushback

YOU WILL LEARN
- How to handle someone's pushback
- Pushback versus attempting to understand

YOU WILL NEED
- 20 minutes to yourself
- Awareness of your body signals
- Writing tools

Everyone has someone in their life who thinks boundaries are, well, suggestions. When we first start setting boundaries, it can be hard for others to adjust to the new normal. You could execute your boundaries perfectly, and someone will *still* push back. This is tricky, and there's no perfect solution. Trust that staying consistent, kind, and firm makes this easier for everyone. You'll need to assess each situation, but let's explore some options.

Use this exercise to evaluate how to handle pushback. Let the explorations guide you, and answer the questions yourself, using a specific situation you may be dealing with:

What's your relationship to the other person? Does their opinion matter to you?

_____

_____

_____

Explore: If you're close to the other person, have faith that healthy relationships can handle renegotiated boundaries. If you're not close to them, ask yourself if their opinion is important.

Are their questions about your boundaries reasonable?

_____

_____

_____

Explore: Sometimes people challenge new boundaries: "Why not?" or "This was fine last week!" You don't owe anyone an explanation, *and* it's helpful to offer compassionate clarification. Some questions are born from genuine curiosity, and it's OK to respond honestly. Try something like "I'm overextended" or "This is what I need to feel safe." Find your own words that capture the same spirit.

What are you really afraid of? Are you currently happy with the relationship?

_____

_____

_____

Explore: What's the consequence you're really afraid of? Abandonment? Being yelled at? Hurting their feelings? Boundaries keep relationships healthy, and secure people respect that. Relationships that crumble due to boundaries are unhealthy; if you need to set boundaries, you're probably already feeling strained. You can't expect others to rejoice in your boundaries, but it's completely reasonable to expect that they will manage their feelings with maturity. If you're setting boundaries with someone immature and reactive, keep it simple and don't overexplain yourself. Pay attention to your body signals. Breathe. Assume best intentions.

What's the most skillful way to hold your boundary?

_____

_____

_____

Explore: You can't control others, but you *can* control yourself. Responding as your best self is the only way to know if the relationship can grow toward security. Here are examples of how you can respond if someone aggressively pushes your boundary:

- *"I understand your concern. I've only realized my need recently, and I'm sharing because you deserve honesty. I'd appreciate your support."*

- *"You don't have to agree. It's OK if you need time to process. I can't stay in this conversation if there's yelling. Think about what I've said, and let's talk when we're calm."*

If someone consistently rages at your boundaries, you may be tired of being the bigger person. I'm not excusing their behavior, but it's still your responsibility (and right!) to enforce your boundaries. If you're constantly taking the lead and seeing no change, it may be time to evaluate whether the relationship is sustainable. We'll go into detail on this later.

5

Trust

Trust is hard for people with anxious attachment. Why trust when the rug isn't bolted to the floor? Let's redefine trust: It's not naively believing what others say or carelessly following their whims. Trust is about generosity—giving the most generous interpretation to events instead of jumping to the worst possible conclusion. We've gone over boundaries and self-regulation, which are the building blocks of self-trust. Next up: exploring tools for trusting others! When you're more focused on your own behavior than what the other person might do, trusting others becomes simple.

Tool 12
Lean on Curiosity

YOU WILL LEARN
- How to be curious
- Curious sentence starters

YOU WILL NEED
- 15 minutes to yourself
- Writing tools

Curiosity is a great way to stop conflict before it starts. When we're curious, we're communicating that we are interested in the other person's perspective. People often argue by speaking for the other person: "So what you're really saying is, it's all my fault! Got it!" An assumption puts someone on the defensive immediately. Curiosity allows room for individual experiences, whereas with assumptions, we presume to know exactly what the other person is thinking. Let's explore how to avoid assuming and lean into curiosity.

How can we use curiosity instead of making an assumption or an accusation? Words like *why* can feel accusatory, and we want this to be a conversation, not a prosecution. "Why did you do that?" will always land more poorly than "Help me understand what happened." Try using some of the following sentence starters, using a recent experience or misunderstanding. Find ways to tweak them to match your authentic voice while maintaining the curious spirit:

Help me understand . . .

"Help me understand what you meant when you made that joke earlier."

Why it works: Asking for help is a way to get the other person on your team, and it comes off as less threatening than just asking why.

Now you try: Help me understand

_____

_____

_____

Tell me more . . .

"Tell me more about what happened for you when I brought up traveling for work."

Why it works: The phrase "tell me more" expresses curiosity without assumption. It communicates, "I'm listening, and I want to know more about your experience."

Now you try: Tell me more

_____

_____

_____

The story I'm telling myself is . . .

"The story I'm telling myself is, you're disappointed in me for taking the project at work that requires more travel. Am I picking up on something or not?"

Why it works: This is a great phrase to use if you find yourself ruminating over your partner's nefarious motives. It takes radical accountability for your part, and it says, "I'm afraid this is what's happening, but I'm willing to be wrong."

Now you try: The story I'm telling myself is

_____

_____

_____

Staying curious means being open and willing to hear the other person and trust their response. It doesn't mean believing someone when their story is outlandish. Still, lead with curiosity whenever possible. Being curious opens the door to conversation and invites the other person to walk through with honesty. This makes it more likely that conflict will go well, which allows the anxious partner to feel more trusting.

Tool 13
Find the Most Generous Interpretation

YOU WILL LEARN
- How to find the most generous interpretation
- Generous reframes

YOU WILL NEED
- 15 minutes to yourself
- Writing tools

Most partners aren't trying to hurt each other—most conflict is a result of misinterpretation. Rather than interpreting your partner's behavior, cultivate a secure relationship by trusting the other person's intentions, giving the benefit of the doubt, and allowing small moments to stay small. This is harder when resentment has built up or if you've had difficult experiences in childhood or past relationships. Let's explore generous reframes for situations with a partner.

You just got home from a long, hard day at work. As you set down your keys, your partner asks from the couch, "What's for dinner tonight?"

Less generous interpretation: *Why is it my job to plan dinner? You've been home for an hour—you deal with it!*

Most generous interpretation: *Hmm, I'm not 100 percent sure why they're asking. Maybe they want something particular.*

Which interpretation is more accurate? You won't know unless you ask, but I can guarantee which one will cause a fight tonight!

If body signals alert that you're having a reaction, pause and fill out the next page. Doing something like filling in the prompts in the moment of a trigger slows down your reaction by creating space for awareness.

If you don't know the answer for certain, ask with curiosity. When we assume the worst, we miss out on the chance to connect authentically. There are always multiple ways to interpret a situation.

In an insecure relationship, resentment builds over time, and we develop a negative perspective of our partner's motives. Sometimes this negative perspective builds from chronic misunderstandings, white lies, or mistrustfulness. This makes it harder to give a generous interpretation, but it's important to know that a negative perspective may be skewed.

Other times, the negative perspective is caused by a big rupture—like the aftermath of an affair, hidden debt, or so on. If that is the case, more specific help, like couples therapy, might be needed to learn to trust again.

If you really believe your partner is deliberately hurting you with no regard for your well-being, I don't recommend staying. You won't know the real answer until you take the lead on changing *your* behavior and see where it goes. For now, giving a more generous interpretation and using curiosity can change the entire emotional tone of a relationship. People who feel trusted feel safe, and emotional safety leads to attachment security.

What objectively happened?
Example: My partner asked what's for dinner.

_____

_____

What is the story I created?
Example: They expect me to take care of dinner after a long day.

_____

_____

What is the meaning I made?
Example: Their time is more valuable than mine.

_____

_____

Is there a more generous interpretation?
Example: Maybe they have a suggestion and want to make sure I didn't already plan something.

_____

_____

Tool 14
The Emotional Bank Account

YOU WILL LEARN
- The importance of the 5:1 ratio
- Bids for connection
- How to respond to bids for connection

YOU WILL NEED
- 15 minutes to yourself
- Writing tools

According to a Gottman Institute study, relationships have an emotional bank account. Each positive interaction between partners deposits one dollar, and like regular bank accounts, it's important to keep a nest egg for hard times. Unfortunately, every negative interaction withdraws five dollars, because bad exchanges hit harder! The heavier weight of negativity means you need five positive interactions to counteract one negative interaction, what is referred to as the 5:1 ratio. Even an equal number of positive and negative interactions will send your bank account into overdraft. Let's explore how to keep that ratio of positive to negative at 5:1.

Upon learning about the 5:1 ratio, people often focus on reducing negative interactions, and that can be the right place to start. Equally important, however, is increasing the positive interactions. An easy way to increase your number of positives is responding to your partner's *bids for connection*.

So what are bids for connection? These are attempts (big and small) to connect with a partner. A bid can be a large olive branch after conflict, a tiny impromptu gesture, or anything in between that says, "I'm thinking about you." Here are some examples:
- Sending a funny meme, reel, or favorite song
- Apologizing
- Reaching out via text or call
- Squeezing your partner's hand
- Bringing home their favorite snack
- Initiating intimacy

There are countless kinds of bids for connection, and it's wise to learn your partner's so you can respond positively. Even anger is often an attempt to pull the other person closer. With that in mind, you can give the most generous interpretation and respond to anger with firm kindness:

"I can see how upset you are. I want to listen, and you deserve to be heard. I can't hear you when there's yelling. Let's take a break and come back in 30 minutes."

Every time you respond to *any* bid for connection with positivity, you're making a deposit in the emotional bank account. You can make it fun. In fact, let's play a connection game: You and your partner will each make five bids for connection over the next week. On Sunday, you'll guess what each other's bids were. Here's how to play:

1. Throughout the week, try to notice the ways your partner is making bids for you. If you're currently not in a relationship, think about a situation with a past partner or love interest. Write down at least five, and think about how you'll respond.

2. Now think about little ways you can show your partner that you care. What would be meaningful to them? Write down five or more. Here are a few examples:

- Offer to watch their favorite show
- Make their favorite meal
- Read that article they sent and talk about it over dinner
- Do a chore for them
- Offer a massage

3. Write your own here:

_____

_____

_____

_____

_____

4. Make those bids to your partner, and keep track of their bids to you.

5. Whoever guesses the most right on Sunday gets quality time of their choice!

Intentionally depositing into the emotional bank account protects your relationship from the negative perspective, encouraging generosity and trust.

Tool 15
Gratitude

YOU WILL LEARN
- Why gratitude is helpful
- Grateful reframes

YOU WILL NEED
- 15 minutes to yourself
- Writing tools

There's no such thing as too much gratitude. We all like to feel appreciated, even for small things. If you're still struggling to make that 5:1 ratio in your relationship, add more gratitude and appreciation. Gratitude isn't just a relational skill; it's scientifically proven to improve our mood. When we find gratitude for small things, we're more likely to feel content. This mental shift can be applied to many aspects of life, and it's a more generous and open way of being.

Imagine this: You've been bickering with your partner recently. The arguments are getting more frequent and heated. Even their chewing annoys you. Maybe they're telling you, "Nothing I do is good enough!" Pause. Whether you agree with your partner or not, their perspective *is* valid. Here's what you can do to increase the gratitude and reap its rewards.

1. Acknowledge their feelings. "I hear you. I've been irritable recently, perhaps unfairly sometimes. Things have been building up for me. Let's talk about it."

2. Reframe your situation using gratitude. Maybe you need more from your partner, and that's fair. But in the meantime, planting seeds of gratitude will cause a more generous relationship to grow. All mammals respond best to positive reinforcement, including you. Let's explore prompts and tips:

   What is my partner getting right? (It's unlikely the answer is truly nothing.)

   _____

   _____

   > Tip: If you want more initiative around chores, notice and praise whenever they get done.

   Which of your partner's qualities do you admire?

   _____

   _____

   > Tip: Remind yourself of why you love them. Intentionally build up your fondness and appreciation.

Is your partner trying to get it right but not quite hitting the mark? What's one example?

_____

_____

> Tip: Praise the effort. "I see you making an effort, and I appreciate it. Thanks for hearing me. What would help the most is [fill in the blank]."

3. Share the tool. You can also do this exercise with a partner. Add these two additional prompts if you're doing this with someone:

   What are five things you currently do for the other person or the relationship?

   _____

   _____

   What are five things you'd like the other person to do for you or the relationship?

   _____

   _____

Now share your answers! Can you both agree to do the things the other person wants you to do?

When partners make an effort to reflect on and communicate fondness and admiration more often, it's more likely that the bond of trust will deepen.

Tool 16
Deepen Your Self-Trust

YOU WILL LEARN
- How to deepen your relationship with yourself
- How to build self-trust

YOU WILL NEED
- 20 minutes to yourself
- Writing tools
- Memory of a tough past event

Trust isn't just for others—it's for yourself, too. Self-regulation and boundaries are important building blocks of self-trust, but it's also helpful to remind yourself of the challenges you've overcome. After all, if you're still here, your track record for surmounting hard times is 100 percent! Sure, it wasn't easy or fun, but you still did it. Be proud of yourself, and frequently remind yourself how far you've come. This tool comes from Yeshiva Davis, a fellow therapist in California who helps professional women balance work and life.

Think of a time you went through emotional pain (heartbreak, betrayal, rejection) and came out stronger. Use Actionable Tip 4, Build Your Relationship with Yourself (page 25), by exploring past experiences to remind yourself of your resilience. Use the example on the next page as a template, but fill in your own answers:

1. What happened? Keep it simple.

   Example: Broke up with my boyfriend

   _____

2. How did you feel at the time?

   Example: Heartbroken, lonely, undesirable

   _____

3. What helped you recover? It's OK if it took longer than you wanted—what worked?

   Example: Meditation, learning to play guitar, hanging out with friends, traveling

   _____

   _____

4. What did you learn about yourself through that experience?

   Example: How to hold my own worth, how to accept it's time to leave a relationship

   _____

   _____

5. Were there any positive changes afterward?

   Example: Lots of personal growth, knowing what I need in relationships going forward

   _____

   _____

Now, apply this to a current pain. Modifying the questions to your situation, ask yourself the following:

1. If I got through something like this before, what's my biggest concern about this current situation?

   Example: I don't want to go through another breakup. I'm disappointed because I wanted this relationship to work. I want to avoid pain. I guess it's going to hurt, but I will actually survive.

   _____

   _____

2. What evidence do I have that I can recover?

   Example: I've been through breakups before. It hurts, but I always eventually move on.

   _____

   _____

3. What helped me last time that I can try again now?

   Example: Learning new skills, spending time with friends, engaging in spirituality, focusing on myself

   _____

   _____

4. Is there something I can do for myself to build trust? What boundaries do I need to set for myself?

   Example: Mute my ex on social media and not look them up, block their number so I'm not tempted to reach out

   _____

   _____

Whatever you're going through relationally, you'll eventually get to the other side. And make sure to set boundaries for yourself and keep them. Boundaries are fertilizer for self-trust. Without boundaries, you'll continue to doubt yourself. With them, you'll grow.

6
Communication

I've hinted previously at the importance of vulnerability, and it's a crucial skill for healthy communication and secure attachment. Vulnerability is how we connect. We can talk with our partner for hours, days, or decades with defensiveness, or we can connect in a heartbeat using vulnerability. Think of vulnerability not as weakness but as getting to the core of the matter instantly. People confuse emotional honesty with vulnerability, but they are not necessarily the same. Telling your partner the reasons you dislike them isn't being vulnerable! To become secure, it's critical to learn to communicate with vulnerability.

Tool 17
Name It to Tame It

YOU WILL LEARN
- Common negative communication styles
- Antidotes to negativity

YOU WILL NEED
- 30 minutes to yourself
- Writing tools

According to the Gottman Institute's research on couples, there are four negative communication styles that are most damaging to use during conflict: criticism, defensiveness, contempt (the most damaging of these), and stonewalling. Dr. Gottman called them the Four Horsemen of the Apocalypse because they signal the end times for a relationship. Thankfully, each negative style has an antidote. This tool will help you identify how you tend to communicate during conflict and how you can improve.

Part 1: The Four Horsemen

The purpose of this exercise is to identify *your* negative communication style, not analyze your partner's. And try to remove judgment—we've all used these communication styles before. Check off those styles you've used, then think of a past fight and describe how you used those negative communication styles.

CRITICISM

- ○ Attacking the other person's character
- ○ Making demands
- ○ Protesting by getting bigger and louder
- ○ Overexplaining your needs
- ○ Feeling urgent and pushing for a response

Example: "I've nagged you three times to load the dishwasher! You're a terrible listener. Just do it!"

_____

_____

DEFENSIVENESS

- ○ Displacing the blame
- ○ Explaining your good intentions without acknowledging their feelings
- ○ Arguing facts
- ○ Playing "blame hot potato"

Example: "All I do is listen to you criticize me! The clean dishes have been put away—I did it at exactly 5 p.m. I'll get to the dirty dishes—relax. If it's so urgent, you do it!"

_____

_____

CONTEMPT
- ○ Name-calling
- ○ Hostile sarcasm
- ○ Scoffing, eye-rolling
- ○ Meanness
- ○ Yelling and raging
- ○ Belittling

Example: "You're a selfish jerk! Everything falls on me! Guess I can look forward to that for the rest of my life. Just go back to work like you always do—at least that's one thing you're good at."

_____

_____

STONEWALLING
- ○ Shutting down and retreating
- ○ Giving the silent treatment
- ○ Passive-aggressively ignoring
- ○ Giving one-word answers
- ○ Withholding affection

Example: "Fine. Whatever. Yes, dear."

_____

_____

Part 2: The Antidote

ANTIDOTES

If you've spotted these horsemen galloping around your relationship situations, try using their antidotes instead. Tone matters here. These messages will work only if your voice and body language are neutral.

Use curiosity.
Example: "Is everything okay? I see that the dishwasher isn't loaded yet."

Take responsibility.
Example: "You're right. I unloaded the clean dishes first, and then an important email popped up. Let me get to that, and then I'll reload the dishwasher right after."

Express fondness/gratitude.
Example: "I appreciate how hard you work. When something isn't getting done, I tell myself that you don't care. It will help me feel heard if you can keep me in the loop when something pops up."

Communicate your need for space.
Example: "Sure, I hear you. Give me 15 minutes, and I'll get on it."

Now write out some antidotes of your own that you can use going forward.

_____

_____

_____

Tool 18
Taking Ownership

YOU WILL LEARN
- How to take ownership for your part
- Three parts to accountability

YOU WILL NEED
- 20 minutes to yourself
- Writing tools
- Memory of a previous conflict

Radical accountability, or taking ownership, is best taken in the moment, but it's also crucial that we come back after conflict to repair. This kind of accountability has three parts: naming how you've contributed, identifying the impact on your partner, and describing how you'll change. It can feel uncomfortable, and that's the point! Vulnerability by definition means you might get hurt. While scary, the risk is worth it for one reason: to know if change is possible.

This exercise is inspired by the work of relationship expert and fellow licensed therapist Julie Menanno, whose book *Secure Love* is another amazing resource for couples wanting to learn how to create attachment security in relationships. Think of the negative behaviors that you've engaged in during conflict with your partner. Do you get urgent and demanding? Are you critical? Do you raise your voice? Use the following example to get started, but think of examples from your own life to fill in the template for yourself.

TEMPLATE

I know that I tend to _____ (criticize, yell) during conflict. Whenever that happens, what I'm really feeling is _____ (desperation for getting my needs met). I know that makes you feel _____ (hurt, attacked). You deserve to feel _____ (heard, respected). I will do better at _____ (being appreciative). It will also help me if _____ (we work as a team).

HERE'S A COMPLETED EXAMPLE

I know that I tend to get angry and enraged during conflict. Whenever that happens, what I'm really feeling is desperate to reach you. I know that makes you feel belittled and pushed away. You deserve to feel safe and cared for. I will do better at taking a break when I get upset. It will also help me if we decide together to come back to talk when we are both ready.

You don't have to follow the template perfectly; use it as a guide. When I give this example, people often ask, "Does anyone really talk like this during conflict?" They do! It may sound strange if you've never had it modeled for you or experienced it yourself. With practice, it will come naturally, and you'll feel more connected and secure.

Tool 19
Assertive Vulnerability

YOU WILL LEARN
- Assertiveness versus aggression
- How to use assertive vulnerability

YOU WILL NEED
- 20 minutes to yourself
- Writing tools

Truly secure communication is vulnerable *and* assertive. Many folks with anxious attachment are people pleasers, so they bottle their feelings until they burst. Admittedly, being vulnerable is harder than suppressing and exploding. What if your partner gets scared off when you share your feelings? I say, let them run! The right person won't run away when you share vulnerability, but most people have trouble receiving an explosion like "You're an idiot!" Let's explore the difference between aggression and assertiveness and how to be vulnerably assertive.

It's common to share feelings honestly and directly but without vulnerability. I know it's a fine line, and it can be confusing in the beginning. You'll know when you've hit the right note. Emotional feedback, for better or worse, is usually instantaneous! Following are templates for assertive vulnerability and examples of how to use them. Think of some examples from your own life, and write out how you might respond:

Aggressive:
"You left the laundry in the washer again! This happens every time. I can't trust you to do the simplest thing!"

Assertive:
"I'm feeling _____ and _____. I really want to _____. Can you help me by _____? That will help me feel _____."

Example:
"I'm feeling disappointed and frustrated. I really want to go down a critical spiral of blame. Can you help me by reassuring me that you understand why I'm upset about the laundry? That will help me feel heard and move on."

Why it works:
When we start by stating a feeling (vulnerability), the other person is less likely to be defensive. Try naming the urge you're feeling—to blame, criticize, defend yourself, and so on. Naming the urge usually takes away its charge. Then ask for help. This increases teamwork and the likelihood that the other person will respond positively.

Aggressive:
"You can't talk to me that way! You're a narcissist!"

Assertive:
"I can't hear you if we're going to _____. It leaves me feeling _____. Let's take a break or start over. What do you think?"

Example:
"I can't hear you if we're going to call each other names. It leaves me feeling disrespected. Let's take a break or start over. What do you think?"

Why it works:
Starting with "I" usually lands better than "You." The first statement sets a boundary without blame, then offers vulnerability. Giving the other person a choice also puts you on the same team and gives them a sense of control. It's also OK to simply state, "I need a break. Let's try again in an hour."

Sentence starters are helpful, but there's no perfect script for vulnerability. However, here are some tips to put you on course:

- Don't take discomfort as a bad sign. Being vulnerable can feel uncomfortable.

- Stay focused on yourself. Share how you're impacted from a place of *self* instead of telling the other person what *they're* doing wrong.

- None of this means you shouldn't stand up to abusive behavior. Unfortunately, however, telling someone they're avoidant, narcissistic, or abusive rarely creates change. If change is possible, the only path is through vulnerability.

Tool 20
Expression Versus Embodiment

YOU WILL LEARN
- The difference between embodiment and expression
- How to express these feelings with vulnerability

YOU WILL NEED
- 20 minutes to yourself
- Writing tools

By now, you probably have a pretty good handle on the anxious attachment behaviors you engage in and their associated body signals. Let's do an exercise that ties them together and gives you a more effective way to express those feelings. Partners are usually responding to our vibe more than our actual feeling. It's safer being confronted with vulnerable feelings than with agitated behavior. By expressing your feelings instead of acting them out, you'll experience better outcomes.

As we've explored, all feelings are tied to body signals, such as a racing heart or a tightened chest. When we feel these signals, we typically get sucked into embodying our feelings through body language, facial expression, and volume. When we're mad, our fists ball up and we might yell. When we're anxious, our heart races and we might become controlling and overbearing. Your partner is more likely to understand your anxious racing heart if it's not embodied through the behaviors of yelling and micromanaging. Let's explore how we can express feelings instead of embodying them.

Using the following examples, fill out the prompts on the next page using your own body signals and communication styles.

Being securely attached isn't about never having anxious feelings anymore; it's about how you communicate that anxiety when it comes up. When we embody our feelings, we may intimidate the other person or attempt to control them with our behavior. All feelings are OK; not all behaviors are. When we learn to express our feelings instead of embodying them, our partner can receive them without defensiveness. As a result, it's more likely that the other person will hear us, our needs will be met, and we will feel secure.

Feeling
Example: Anger, frustration

___

Body signal
Example: Feeling hot, heart racing

___

Communication style
Example: Criticism, protesting, and demanding

___

Embodiment
Example: Yelling, scoffing, rushing around

___

Expression
Example: "I'm feeling frustrated we're running late. Can we set aside more time to get ready in the future?"

___

___

___

Feeling
Example: Anxiety

_____

Body signal
Example: Heart racing, fidgeting

_____

Communication style
Example: Criticism, defensiveness, blaming

_____

Embodiment
Example: Snapping, micromanaging

_____

Expression
Example: "My anxiety is high, and I really want to be controlling. Can we go over the list together to make sure we didn't forget anything?"

_____

_____

_____

Tool 21
Validation

YOU WILL LEARN
- How to validate feelings
- What validation is and isn't

YOU WILL NEED
- 20 minutes to yourself
- Writing tools

Want your partner to validate your feelings more often? Take the lead and validate theirs! The best way to get more of anything in a relationship is to model it yourself and praise your partner when you see it happening. If their experience conflicts with your own, validating theirs can feel like saying something untrue. Maybe it feels like an admission of guilt when you're innocent. Whatever the reason, it's important to know that validation is a necessary relational skill. The more easily you can validate the other person's perspective, the quicker conflict will generally resolve.

How can I validate something invalid? Everyone leaves the toilet seat up! You're not validating facts; you're validating feelings. Emotions are always valid, and we're not making up our experience. However, feelings don't always reflect objective reality (I don't recommend reminding your partner of this during fights).

Feelings come through the lens of our personal history and core beliefs; hence, they are usually muddied by our interpretation. Writer Anaïs Nin explains this beautifully: "We don't see things as they are, we see them as *we* are." So, it's quite possible that you're innocent *and* your partner feels hurt by you. Both can be true simultaneously.

If your partner isn't giving you a generous interpretation, the quickest way out of a fight is to validate their feelings, even if you disagree. Here's a template to get you started:

> "I can see why you're feeling _____. This has been _____ in the past, so your [feeling] is understandable. That's not where I'm coming from right now. Are you open to hearing _____?"
>
> **Example:**
> *"I can see why you're feeling manipulated. This has been a painful topic for us in the past, so your mistrust is understandable. That's not where I'm coming from right now. Are you open to hearing my thoughts?"*
>
> **Why it works:**
> By acknowledging the difficulty or history around the topic, you're letting the other person know that you see their experience as important, too. Asking if you can share your thoughts is nondefensive and allows the other person to say no if they aren't ready.

Using an example from your own relationship, write a message of validation here:

_____

_____

Helpful tips

- Feeling accused? Don't fight about details—find the feeling and validate it. Try saying, "I can see why you feel that way; that makes sense. I hear you."
- Validation is never an admission of guilt but rather acknowledgment that you hear the other person and care about their experience. Try not to get stuck on proving your innocence or being "right."
- Acknowledge how the relationship's past impacts the current moment. Have you been defensive in the past? State that you see how that could be influencing your partner now.
- Validation doesn't mean accepting verbal abuse, name-calling, and so on. That's what boundaries are for. Still, you can validate while setting boundaries: "You're upset at me; I hear you. I can't stay in this conversation with name-calling. I'm taking a break and will be back in an hour."

Tool 22
Write It Out

YOU WILL LEARN
- How to get your feelings out
- How to translate vulnerability

YOU WILL NEED
- 30 minutes to yourself
- Writing tools

As mentioned earlier, those with anxious attachment often want co-regulation, meaning they're looking for someone else to give them the attunement they lacked as a child. Unfortunately, others can't always give what we're looking for.

If you feel like you're going to explode at someone in an attempt to feel heard, grab a piece of paper or writing app and write out your feelings instead.

The number-one rule for this letter is DO NOT SEND. I'm serious—please don't send this as an email, text, or Morse code. This is purely for the purpose of venting your feelings. If you send this to anyone, I fear you will surely regret it later.

EXAMPLE (UNEDITED) LETTER
"I hate it when you don't call at the time we agreed on. You make me feel worthless and crazy. I don't know why I even try. You're a selfish, immature jerk! I just want you to keep your promises—is that so much to ask? It takes 10 seconds to shoot a text, but you won't even do that. You're too busy thinking of yourself and not considering me at all."

Once you've written the letter, take some time to sit with your feelings. Do a self-regulating activity, like breathing, exercise, or holding an ice cube. Then, from a calmer place, ask yourself: *What's under the surface of my frustration? Hurt? Fear?* How can you express that instead by using the communication skills you've learned?

When you're ready, revisit or rewrite the letter, making edits for vulnerability.

It might look like this:

> "I know I've been critical about this in the past, so I understand why it's hard for us to talk about. I can be demanding during conflict. Whenever that happens, what I'm really feeling is desperate to be heard. I know that makes you feel pressured and responsible for my feelings. You deserve to feel safe and unburdened. I will do better at being less demanding when I'm upset. It will also help me if we can keep agreements we've made to each other. When I don't hear from you on time, I worry about your safety and our relationship, and that leaves me feeling unworthy of the effort to text me. I will feel safer if you can shoot me a quick text letting me know you're running late. Can we work on this together?"

Sit with this new, kinder letter. When you're ready, share this version with your partner *in person* by reading it aloud. Do not send it via email or text. So much social context is lost when you don't speak in person. In general, I don't recommend talking about difficult topics by text—it is always better to use your voice and presence.

PART III

Being Secure in Love

These tools are nice, but I don't understand how to use them in real situations!
How do I know if I'm meeting someone emotionally available?
Can this situation actually get better?

Most of us weren't taught how to date, recognize a healthy relationship, or break up. Now that we've gone over tools to help you build security, let's explore how to apply these tools during the different stages of love: dating, maintaining relationships, and breaking up. My goal in this next section is to provide a road map for tough, everyday situations by sharing examples. While many of these scenarios are based on my clinical experience, none of them are actual client stories.

I know that real-life application is always the hardest! It's one thing to read about a tool and another to use it when you get that midnight text that says, "You up?" Be patient with yourself as you learn to apply your new knowledge.

7
Dating and Looking for Love
(in All the Wrong Places)

Dating is inherently nerve-racking for the anxiously attached. In the beginning phases of dating, you're met with an anxious person's worst nightmare: *uncertainty*. I often hear, "I *hate* dating! I just want to feel settled." I remember that feeling—it's not fun! Unfortunately, anxious people often rush to create feelings of safety. My advice is this: Be patient. The dating phase is massively important; it's how you get to know someone and if they're the right fit for you. If you rush through, you'll commit to someone before you actually know them, and you'll end up in that old, tired dynamic.

Situation 1: Pedal to the Floor

Jenna is 31, creative, fun, bright, and looking for a serious relationship. After a few dates with a new man, she finds herself imagining their future. She daydreams about buying a house, traveling, and all the special moments they'll have together. When he doesn't text back within several hours of her reaching out, she starts to ruminate. *Why hasn't he texted yet? Is it over?* She wants commitment, and if the new guy isn't ready after a few weeks, she's disappointed. She wonders, *What's wrong with me? Why won't anybody commit?*

What's Really Going On?

Jenna is applying relationship expectations to the dating phase. Dating isn't about picturing your life together; it's about getting to know the other person. Are they reliable and respectful? Do your values align? It's normal during the dating phase to see multiple people. You can focus on one person if you decide you want a relationship with them down the road, but I don't recommend committing after just a few good dates. Take your time. You don't fully know someone until you see them when they've had a bad day. Or when they're angry. Or when they're angry at *you*. After that, you'll know better if they're worth the investment.

Address the Issue

1. Remember Actionable Tip 2, Be Patient (page 23). When you don't get an immediate response, first remember, this is not an emergency. Slow down and notice your body signals, then use Tool 1, Trigger Map (page 31), to identify why you're feeling this way.

2. Now that you've recognized your body signals, use Tool 3, Breathing Exercises (page 37); Tool 4, Sensory Soothing (page 40); or Tool 5, Move Your Body (page 43)—whatever works for you. If you're at work, choose something you can do at your desk, like breathing. Set a timer for two or more minutes and dedicate your full attention to your self-care.

3. Once you're calmer, self-validate with Tool 2 (page 34). Take a moment to write down some validating phrases, such as "I'm anxious to get to the next phase, and I want to push. It's OK if uncertainty is still hard for me. Even if I never hear back from him, I'll be OK. I was OK before him; I'll be OK after him."

4. Use Tool 9 (page 56) to consider a more reasonable expectation of this situation. This might look like, *We're still getting to know each other. I don't know him well enough to imagine a future together. He doesn't owe me lightning-fast responses yet.*

Discussion Notes: Does following this plan mean you'll have no anxiety about the situation? Probably not. But it's your best bet to help you slow down and not resort to rushing or pushing to get the response you want. Dating and getting to know someone takes time. Let the process breathe.

Situation 2: Hooking Up

Andre is in his mid-20s. He does casual hookups sometimes (all of his friends are doing it), but he secretly longs for a deeper connection and doesn't really enjoy just hooking up. He worries that he's the only young gay man like this (he isn't!), so he has a hard time telling dates what he's really looking for. What if they judge him? Shouldn't he want to be spontaneous and free like the rest of his friends?

What's Really Going On?

Online hookup culture is huge. It's one of the biggest issues people bring to therapy. While some enjoy it, many go along with it even though it doesn't align with their ultimate values. It's important to have fun while dating, but always stay in touch with what you truly want. And don't be afraid of scaring anyone away. The sooner the wrong person leaves, the sooner you can make room for the right person! If someone disappears after you set a boundary, especially around sex, then you know that's all they wanted anyway. If that's not all you're looking for, try not to see this as a rejection. Your relationship goals simply didn't match, and that's important if you're looking for something long-term. Andre's worried about scaring people away or being seen as "not [fill in the blank] enough." He'll take the intimacy of a hookup over nothing, even if it's not what he really wants. This dynamic happens in all kinds of relationships.

Address the Issue

1. If you want something more serious than casual sex, start by taking radical accountability! Actionable Tip 1 (page 22) can remind you how to do this. "I don't want to move too fast. I'm looking for a long-term, monogamous relationship."

2. Do you need a confidence boost to express yourself? Use Tool 2 to self-validate (page 34). Remind yourself, *I'm allowed to want a serious relationship. Some people enjoy hooking up, and some don't. It's good to know what I want.*

3. Finally, communicate skillfully with new dates using assertive vulnerability (Tool 19, page 91). If someone makes a move before you're ready to be intimate, try something like "That sounds really fun, but not tonight" or "I'm attracted to you, but I prefer more connection before we get physical."

Discussion Notes: If you want to have casual sex, go for it! Just be safe and responsible. But also be honest with yourself: Do you get more attached once you're physical? Are you hoping sex will make the other person like you more? If so, set yourself up for success by waiting a little longer to make sure you're getting attached to someone who's aligned with you.

Situation 3: Being a Rescue Ranger

Miguel is a kind man in his 30s with a history of choosing partners who need "rescuing." His girlfriends can't keep down a job, or they're late on rent or bills, and it's always someone else's fault. He wants to be understanding, so he pours time, effort, and money into new relationships to show his loyalty. Soon, it becomes clear there's a deeper issue going on—addiction or a mental health diagnosis that's untreated. Miguel has a big heart, but he's overgiving; maybe if he just loves them enough, they'll get better. Unfortunately, it never works, and he's left feeling used, confused, and alone when the relationship eventually implodes.

What's Really Going On?

This is codependence, and it comes down to self-worth. Miguel witnessed his mother caretake for his father, so this dynamic feels familiar to him. If you grew up in a similar situation or have a history of dating people struggling with addiction, take your time getting to know someone, and pay attention to red flags, like someone's inability to keep a job or constant need to borrow money. Miguel hopes that by showing up consistently for someone, they'll reciprocate. If you're constantly giving and not seeing any change, you may have unreasonable expectations. This approach also puts the giver in a "savior" role, which creates a hierarchy and doesn't allow a relationship of equals.

Address the Issue

1. Revisit Actionable Tip 1, Take Radical Accountability (page 22). What is Miguel's part? For starters, he's enabling his partner's behavior by not setting limits.

2. Take some time to identify your needs by filling out the table in Tool 7 (page 50). What do you need to feel loved? Are those needs being met?

3. Next, use Tool 10, Understanding Guilt (page 59), to ask yourself, *Does setting a boundary feel painful?* Are you worried about the other person's well-being at the cost of your own? Reframe guilt using your values. *Feeling guilty doesn't mean I'm doing anything wrong. I'm not empowering anyone to take accountability for their own life if I'm constantly rescuing them. I'm not doing this to be mean; I'm doing it to prevent resentment.*

4. Finally, set boundaries with vulnerability, and prepare for pushback (Tool 11, page 62). You can't control another person's reaction, so control your own: "I care about you so much, and I want you to get the help you need. I'm worried your needs are beyond my ability at this point. I can't lend more money at this time. You need help from someone experienced in managing addiction."

Discussion Notes: Addiction and mental health are very painful, sensitive topics. I understand why it's hard to set boundaries with someone you love. The purpose of boundaries isn't to be unkind but actually to preserve the relationship. The road to breakups is often paved with resentment, but boundaries prevent bitterness. For their part, people with an addiction have to be ready to change for themselves. All the love in the world won't convince them.

Situation 4: *Shrinking Yourself*

Lauren is an intelligent, ambitious woman in her mid-20s, finishing up law school. She worries that men are intimidated by her, so she tries to play it cool. A date ghosts her for three weeks, then texts out of nowhere late at night, "Hey, sorry, I've been busy. Wanna hang out?" She says, "Sure, why not?" and goes over, hoping that his behavior will change if she's super chill (spoiler alert—it doesn't!). He keeps asking to see her, so he must like her, right? But he never takes her out. He usually just invites her over to his place to "hang out." She's shrinking herself in hopes of being liked, but she's left feeling frustrated and unfulfilled.

What's Really Going On?

Lauren thinks, *But I really like him! We have chemistry, and he's giving me mixed messages, so maybe he's just confused.* Ask yourself, do you actually like *them*, or the idea of them? Do you like what *could* be if they just changed their behavior? It's wise to take people as they are, especially in the beginning phases of dating. This is how you vet someone to make sure you have the same goals. Chemistry might be fun in the moment, but it can also blow up the lab. Sparks don't make a relationship sustainable, and they're not the sign that this is a long-term relationship. If you want a relationship, look for shared values, such as reliability, honesty, work ethic, thoughtfulness, and kindness. Is the other person exhibiting characteristics that you respect, or do you just want their attention?

Address the Issue

1. Use Tool 19, Assertive Vulnerability (page 91), to communicate your needs and boundaries. "I'm looking for someone who wants to see me consistently to potentially build a relationship. What are you looking for?"

2. Not sure what the other person is really asking? Let them know! Enlist curiosity using Tool 12 (page 67). "Tell me more about what you mean when you say 'hang out'? If you're asking me on a date, sure! When and where were you thinking?" While the beginning stages of dating can be uncertain, you deserve to feel certain that someone's interested.

3. If the other person asks you to "hang out" or come over to their place at the last minute, set a boundary using Tool 6 (page 47), for guidance. This can look like "I'd like to see you, but I'm looking to go out for a nice evening. Let me know if you'd like to plan something. Otherwise, I'll pass tonight."

Discussion Notes: If you shrink yourself to be liked, you're engaging in a negative cycle of communication, which doesn't give the other person the chance to show up for you, if they're capable. Shrinking yourself also isn't really connecting—it's hiding. You deserve to be yourself and not pretend you don't have needs to keep the peace. The point of relationships isn't peace; it's connection, and connection requires honest vulnerability.

Situation 5: Texting Anxiety

Online dating and apps have changed dating culture significantly. Besides hookup culture, a common issue people bring to me is "texting anxiety," or not understanding the rules and expectations of how often to text a new person. Sol is a nonbinary person who struggles to get dates to materialize. They receive messages, but it's awkward texting with a stranger, and conversation fizzles before a date gets scheduled. Sol feels pressure to say the right thing, so they end up overthinking and shutting down. They're worried they're texting too much or too little, and that's part of why dates aren't happening.

What's Really Going On?

It's important to know that texting isn't really connecting with someone new. Texting gives the false impression that you know the other person. It's also easy to drift apart via text because there's low investment, and there's always someone new to message. We might not know what to say, or we may have different expectations for texting than the other person. Sol struggles in part because they get stuck in their own head about whether or not the other person likes them, and they're unsure how to assert their desire to meet in person. So, they stay quiet, hoping the other person will take the lead. Just go on a date! That's how you authentically connect with someone new.

Address the Issue

1. Remember Actionable Tip 3, Take the Lead (page 24). If you want an in-person date, ask for one! At the very least, open the door for the other person to ask. If the conversation is flowing or an interesting topic comes up, try "I'm enjoying this conversation. Should we continue in person?"

2. Assertive vulnerability (Tool 19, page 91) can help you communicate what you actually want with vulnerability and without blame. This might look like "I'm enjoying chatting, and I'd like to schedule something in person. What do you think?"

3. Finally, try to give the most generous interpretation (Tool 13, page 70). Don't assume what the other person is thinking; just ask if you're unsure! "Are you looking to meet in person? How's this weekend for you?"

Discussion Notes: It's easy to fall into overthinking. Try not to take slow responses or even ghosting personally at this stage. For some people, texting is extremely low stakes, and they aren't yet invested. If you really want to see if there's relationship potential, try to meet as soon as possible instead of texting for days or weeks.

Situation 6: Situationships

Bailey has been strung along for six months with no commitment. When she asks the person she's been seeing about their future, he replies, "I don't like expectations. Let's see where it goes." He treats her like a girlfriend—they go on real dates, he plans little getaways, and he might even say, "I love you." Usually, the sexual connection in these kinds of relationships is very exciting. But whenever she needs emotional support or asks what they're doing in the long term, he becomes cold and distant. Bailey's confused. On one hand, it seems like he's interested; on the other, something's missing.

What's Really Going On?

Modern dating is rife with situationships. We all probably have that friend in a pseudo-relationship with no labels and no boundaries who texts screenshots of their conversations, asking you to help them decipher the deeper meaning. Sometimes, *you* are that friend! If you set one dating goal for yourself for this year, let it be this: No more situationships! These kinds of relationships usually contain something very addictive: intermittent approval. Think of intermittent approval like gambling. You're playing the slot machine, and occasionally, you hit it big. *Holy cow, this is amazing!* So, you play again; this time, you lose. So, you play again. That rush of *What if I win again?* is addictive. Every time you "win" the other person's attention, you're flooded with attachment hormones like oxytocin and dopamine. The problem is, you're probably losing more than you're winning, and you're betting on someone who isn't looking for the commitment jackpot.

Address the Issue

1. Two actionable tips can be used here: 1, Take Radical Accountability (page 22), and 4, Build Your Relationship with Yourself (page 25). Ask yourself, *How am I contributing to this cycle? Am I staying when my needs aren't being met? How can I choose myself in this situation? What do I actually want?*

2. Enlist some self-validation (Tool 2, page 34) and remind yourself that your expectations aren't unreasonable. *Commitment after three months of dating isn't unreasonable. My needs aren't too much, but I may be asking from someone who isn't capable of giving.*

3. Don't ask the other person to change. State your boundary, and pay attention to their willingness to change (or not). Use Boundaries Versus Requests (Tool 6, page 47) to guide you. "We've been dating for three months. For me, that's long enough to know whether you want to be committed. To feel safe and loved in this relationship, I need commitment at this point. If you're not interested, then we're not a match."

Discussion Notes: Sometimes, you have to break your own heart. It's disappointing when you're not aligned with someone you really like. While setting boundaries can mean the other person will leave, it's the best way to build your relationship with yourself. Boundaries are about holding our own self-worth, which breeds self-respect. Increased self-respect becomes self-love, and that's a huge piece of secure attachment.

Situation 7: Red Flags

Ynez is a queer woman in her 50s looking for a relationship. She's recently divorced and afraid of experiencing that pain again. When she gets a new match on Bumble, she finds all the things wrong with the other woman or her message. "Can you believe she asked me out to coffee?" she tells a friend. "Show some effort! At least ask me to dinner." She's sabotaging her chance of the best date of her life before it even starts.

What's Really Going On?

If you've been hurt before, it's easy to become hypervigilant and see red flags everywhere. Ynez is creating red flags with her self-protective attitude! I understand why Ynez sees dating through a negative filter—putting yourself out there is vulnerable, especially when you've had bad experiences. At the same time, you won't avoid pain by closing yourself off from meeting or talking to new people. You'll just feel the pain of loneliness instead. You're swapping the risk of vulnerability for the risk of isolation. While there's nothing wrong with being alone, make that choice intentionally and not out of fear of being hurt. If you want a relationship, you can't avoid discomfort. It's inevitable—all relationships contain some suffering. But choosing the right relationship can make even suffering feel productive and worthwhile.

Address the Issue

1. First, take radical accountability (Actionable Tip 1, page 22). Are you being exceptionally negative or closed off? How can you change your behavior to make yourself more open?

2. Try using self-validation (Tool 2, page 34). Own your feelings so they don't dictate your behavior. *I'm nervous about meeting new people. I want to pick apart the other person and find all the reasons not to go out with them to protect myself. It's OK if I'm scared; I can take things slowly.*

3. Next, use the gift of Tool 15, Gratitude (page 76). Maybe you've been disappointed in the past, or relationships haven't gone the way you've hoped. Has anything gone right? Did you learn any lessons from those experiences? What's going right in your life at this moment? Finding gratitude for what you have will put you in a better headspace, and that will make it easier to open up and meet new people.

4. Finally, set reasonable expectations with Tool 9 (page 56). Coffee *is* a reasonable first date to propose. If you would prefer something else and it's that important to you, take the lead (page 24) and suggest it! "I'd prefer drinks or dinner. What do you think?"

Discussion Notes Try not to get hung up on something small before you've met someone. You don't know them yet, so how do you know if you won't like them? If there's no glaring issue, I recommend going on a quick date (an hour or so) just to catch the vibe. And yeah, it might be awkward at first—if you want instant chemistry, watch a rom-com. As long as there's no bright red flag waving, go on another date. Sometimes it takes a few dates to build a connection, and some people are shy at first. Give people a chance, and you may be pleasantly surprised!

Situation 8: Rose-Colored Glasses

Jasmine is turning 40 this year, and she's longing to start a family. She feels short on time to realize this dream, so when a new guy expresses strong interest, she thinks, *Finally, a man not scared of commitment!* On their second date, he starts planning their future, asking, "You're not still talking to other guys, right?" He boasts about making enough money to take care of them, so she shouldn't keep her job. He'll take care of everything! He's generous and charming, bringing her to luxury stores to shop, but he also wants her to commit immediately. Jasmine is eager to settle down, so she's hopeful this man is "the one," but she's missing subtle cues—actually red flags—that he may be controlling and jealous.

What's Really Going On?

Getting to know someone new can be intoxicating. However, just as you shouldn't drive drunk on alcohol, you shouldn't make a huge commitment (like marriage and children) drunk on infatuation. Wait until you've sobered up! The purpose of dating is to learn about someone over time in a variety of situations. If you don't know how this person manages conflict, you don't know if your values are aligned enough to parent together. Questioning if you're dating other people after a date or two is often a red flag. The point of dating is to spend time with people and explore who's the right fit before settling into a relationship. Be cautious of people too eager to move quickly. Sometimes they're attempting to dazzle you before you realize something's wrong.

Address the Issue

1. Be patient (Actionable Tip 2, page 23). Take your time getting to know someone new. There's no rush. I know it's hard if you want a family, but having children with the wrong person could end up being worse!

2. Next, enlist reasonable expectations (Tool 9, page 56). Getting married and having a family in a very short amount of time may not be a reasonable expectation for yourself or anyone else. Healthy families are built on secure attachment, and this takes time.

3. Use Tool 12, Lean on Curiosity (page 67). If someone wants to move very quickly or is asking you to commit after a date or two, get curious. "Help me understand, why do you want to commit this early?"

4. If necessary, set boundaries with assertive vulnerability (Tool 19, page 91). "I'm enjoying getting to know you, and I'm also looking for a serious relationship. But I need more

time. Let's check in again on this discussion at the end of the month."

Discussion Notes: Sometimes people are just excited about a new relationship, and there's no malicious intent to control—but sometimes there is. You won't know until you give it more time. Research shows that couples who wait a minimum of three to five years before getting married have happier, longer-term marriages. This is because they actually know the other person! It's easy to hide your flaws for a few months and much harder to hide them for three to five years.

8
Relationships and Maintaining Love

We are hurt in relationships, and we heal in relationships. Yes, attachment work requires significant individual effort, but many attachment wounds need to be worked out with another person. So, how do you maintain relationships when you get stuck in your attachment dynamic? The good news is, doing your part differently can drastically change the emotional quality of the relationship, even if your partner doesn't change certain things. When you change, the other person changes in your eyes. Often, that's good enough.

Situation 9: Demanding Honesty

People commonly confuse honesty and vulnerability, but as we explored in chapter 6, they're not necessarily the same. Suze is in her 30s and living with her long-term boyfriend, Cal. Suze has her closet color-coordinated, which helps her stay calm. Cal has his "closet" scattered across their bedroom floor. Suze believes she's sharing feelings when she says, "I feel like your maid! You're such a slob." If he doesn't hop to cleaning immediately, she becomes impatient and demanding. "This is so annoying! Just do it!" Cal becomes defensive when Suze gets loud. He feels attacked and like he's given no grace.

What's Really Going On?

Should Cal pick up after himself? Absolutely! Suze's frustration is valid, but she's not communicating using the most skillful means: vulnerability. You (or Suze) may ask, "Can't I just say how I feel?" Yes, but "I feel like your maid" is not a feeling. Effective communication means naming specific emotions, like feeling disappointed or overwhelmed. If your sentence starts with "I feel like you . . . ," you're probably sharing criticism or contempt instead of a vulnerable feeling. The way we say things matters. It can feel inauthentic not to express yourself as bluntly as you want, but it's better for the relationship to stay respectful and generous, even when you're totally frustrated with your partner. There's a way to say almost anything that is kind *and* authentic.

Address the Issue

1. Start with Actionable Tip 3, Take the Lead (page 24). Try to start every conversation about cleaning (or whatever it is) using the most skillful communication you can muster. You will feel better, and your partner is more likely to hear you.

2. Move your body (Tool 5, page 43). If you're easily frustrated, engage in some movement to calm down before saying anything to the other person. It's much easier to be kind when you're calm.

3. The next time you need to talk about cleaning (or whatever it is), start with the template from Tool 18, Taking Ownership (page 89). "I know that I tend to be critical and demanding during conflict. Whenever that happens, what I'm really feeling is desperate to be heard. I know that makes you feel attacked and belittled. I will do better at being more vulnerable instead of embracing anger and frustration. It will also help me if you can tell me when you'll get to my requests."

4. Do you think your partner leaves stuff around the house because they think it's your job to pick it up? Or do you think it's because they're overwhelmed? Find a more generous interpretation (Tool 13, page 70) and you'll both feel better!

Discussion Notes: A whopping 70 percent of conflict in relationships is recurring, meaning it can't be solved and will continue to pop up, according to a 1999 study by Gottman and Levenson. This cycle of conflict is due to a difference in personalities: One person is neat; the other's messy. One is spontaneous; the other's a planner. You're not going to change your partner from being spontaneous to being a planner. Instead, find a way to talk about your differences constructively. One of the best ways to do that is to maintain respectful communication, even if you're frustrated.

Situation 10: I Only Have Eyes for You

Anya and Julian just got engaged after three years together. They met playing Ultimate Frisbee, and they still love playing together on a team. Recently, Anya has begun thinking that Julian is looking at other women on the field. He swears he isn't ogling anyone; he's just watching people play, like he's always done. He tries to reassure her, but Anya gets so upset that she storms off during a game. A tornado of accusations ensues in the car: "You're gaslighting me! I saw you staring!"

What's Really Going On?

Gaslighting is a term I hear frequently, so let's define it. Disagreeing with your partner isn't gaslighting. Even saying "that's not what happened" isn't necessarily gaslighting (it's defensiveness). Gaslighting is intentional, malicious manipulation. It's rare. Most partners are not gaslighting each other, but they are lost in their own painful perspectives. Anya's mother cheated on her father and abandoned the family. If you grew up in a family or were part of a relationship that involved an affair or serious dishonesty and infidelity, be careful that your mind isn't playing tricks on you. It's easy to project our previous relationships onto our partners.

Address the Issue

1. If you're upset enough to burst, take a moment to remind yourself that this isn't actually an emergency. Your partner isn't going to run off immediately if you don't intervene. Remind yourself to be patient (Actionable Tip 2, page 23), and then use some breathing exercises (Tool 3, page 37), to calm your body.

2. Your feelings make sense given your history. It's OK to feel the way you do; however, your current behaviors may be ineffective. Tool 2 (page 34) can help you validate yourself. You might start with *I'm afraid of being abandoned. I'm just scared. It's OK to be afraid.*

3. Partners respond better to vulnerable feelings than accusations. Revisit Tool 19, Assertive Vulnerability (page 91), for guidance to respond this way: "I'm feeling insecure and hurt, like I want to accuse you of looking at other women. Can you help by reassuring me that you only want to be with me? That will help me feel safe."

4. Since you see things so differently, validating the other person's perspective (Tool 21, page 99) will help. "I can see why you feel accused and anxious when I bring up looking at other women. This has been painful for us in the past, so your fear is understandable. That's not where I'm coming from right now. Are you open to hearing my fears?"

Discussion Notes A crucial detail in this example: Julian really *isn't* looking inappropriately at other women. If one partner is genuinely being disrespectful, that would be a different situation with a different action plan. It's human to notice when others are attractive, even if you've been partners for years! What matters is what we do with that attraction. Simply glancing at someone you find attractive is not infidelity, but if it bothers one of you, talk about it respectfully and with vulnerability.

Situation 11: Rejection

Tomas and Charlotte are in their 40s and have two kids. They've been married 12 years, and they're stuck in a pursuer-withdrawer dynamic in their sex life. Tomas misses the closeness of intimacy, but Charlotte says no almost every time he reaches for her. She's always too tired, stressed, or busy. Although he tries to be respectful when turned down, sometimes he feels hurt and rejected. Whenever he brings up the topic, Charlotte accuses him of only wanting sex. Tomas feels misunderstood, disconnected, and desperate to reach his wife again.

What's Really Going On?

Sex is a tricky topic. The most important rule of a healthy sexual relationship is that all sexual activity must be 100 percent consensual. If someone doesn't want intimacy, then it shouldn't be happening between you. If you're in a similar situation as Tomas or Charlotte, the issue probably isn't actually sex. Most likely, a deeper attachment need isn't being met, but it's manifesting as a lack of sexual intimacy. Maybe Charlotte feels overburdened and that Tomas isn't helping enough with the kids. Maybe they're not spending enough quality time together. The best way to deal with this situation is not to address sex directly but, instead, to work on their emotional connection.

Address the Issue

1. Instead of taking it personally, take the lead (Actionable Tip 3, page 24) in trying to understand why your partner doesn't want intimacy lately. Seek to understand the emotions. Pouting about or demanding sex will never get the desired result.

2. Acknowledge Tool 8, Respecting Others' Boundaries (page 53). If your partner doesn't want intimacy, it's necessary to honor that. You can say, "I hear you—you're not interested in sex right now, and I respect your wishes. At some point, I'd like to have a longer conversation about why we're not connecting that way anymore. It's an important topic to me, and I want to hear your perspective, too."

3. Curiosity is not an interrogation of "why?!" Instead, it might look like "The story I'm telling myself is that you don't want to have sex anymore because you're not attracted to me. Can you reassure me that isn't the reason?" Be curious (Tool 12, page 67) to demonstrate genuine interest in what your partner is thinking and why.

4. Finally, check in with Tool 14, the Emotional Bank Account (page 73). Tomas is making a bid for connection with sexual intimacy. But Charlotte may well be making other bids for connection to Tomas that he's not hearing. Their disconnection may come from misreading each other's bids. Noticing the ways your partner is reaching out to you improves emotional intimacy, and that just might lead to great sex.

Discussion Notes: For some people, sexual connection equals emotional connection. Others need emotional connection before being able to have sex. It's common for partners to have mismatched sex drives and for sex to mean different things to each of them. Don't try to interpret your partner's behavior; instead, get curious and seek to understand them as an act of love. You'll both feel better understood and respected.

Situation 12: In Hot Pursuit

Lee is in their 30s, and when they have conflict with their partner, Nina, they'll follow her around the house demanding to talk. If Nina asks for space, Lee can't give it. If Nina leaves the house, Lee blows up her phone with angry messages. Nina expresses how overwhelmed she feels by Lee's anger, but Lee gets stuck in self-righteous justification. "She just disappears!" Lee complains. "If I don't chase after her, she won't talk about anything!"

What's Really Going On?

When an anxiously attached person is triggered and upset, they can become an "angry pursuer," meaning they may push to talk because they can't tolerate disconnection. For many anxiously attached folks, the fear of abandonment develops into anger. The problem is, anger doesn't pull anyone closer—it pushes them away. Nina also plays a role by withdrawing, but it's still Lee's responsibility to control their own reaction. Intense outward anger often protects equally intense inward shame. Feelings of self-righteousness or justification may be at the surface in the moment, but they're just anger in a different mask. As soon as they fade, you're left feeling guilty, embarrassed, and ashamed. Figure out what's underneath all that anger and what you're hoping to achieve. Find ways to express that instead. Once you understand what purpose anger is serving, you'll have a much easier time managing it.

Address the Issue

1. No one else can calm you down, but radical accountability can help get you started so you can self-regulate and handle your emotions. Start with Actionable Tip 1 and take radical accountability (page 22).

2. Next, build a trigger map (Tool 1, page 31). What are the specific things that trigger you, and why? What is your first body signal? The moment you feel that signal light up, use a self-soothing tool that works for you, such as breathing (Tool 3, page 37), sensory soothing (Tool 4, page 40), or movement (Tool 5, page 43). Sensory soothing can be

especially helpful when you're stirred up. If you want to say something mean, put something strongly flavored in your mouth. Keep gum or sour candies in your pocket for quick access.

3. Anger is a healthy emotion when expressed in healthy ways. It's OK to be angry—it's not OK to take anger out on your partner. Fill out the table in Tool 20, Expression Versus Embodiment (page 95), and brainstorm ways to communicate assertively instead of aggressively.

4. Finally, identify your negative communication style with Tool 17, Name It to Tame It (page 85). Do you become contemptuous and mean? Critical and demanding? What's the antidote to your negative style? How can you use it during conflict?

Discussion Notes: People with anxious attachment usually want co-regulation, or to calm down with the other person. Unfortunately, your partner may be someone who gets hives from co-regulation and desperately wants alone time to self-regulate. Both of these are necessary relational skills, and you'll have to find a balance together. That said, expecting any partner to hold space for severe anger directed at them is unreasonable. If you're anxiously attached, focus first on self-soothing, and then come to your partner with vulnerability.

Situation 13: Ethical Nonmonogamy

Isabel and her partner Jeremy have opened their relationship. They've had many conversations about boundaries and communication, and they both feel on the same page. Since they've started dating other people, Isabel is noticing jealousy creep in. When Jeremy leaves for the evening, she questions him obsessively. How long will he be out? Is he more attracted to this new person? Jeremy answers her questions patiently, but Isabel feels guilty. She can't calm her anxiety and doesn't feel better until Jeremy is home. She wants to feel happy for Jeremy's new connections, like he is for hers, but she's wracked with fear that he'll leave her for someone else.

What's Really Going On?

Opening a relationship can bring up a lot of feelings. Sometimes it's hard to know exactly how you'll feel until you're in it. While nonmonogamy is a valid relational style, it doesn't solve relationship problems and can be particularly challenging for people with anxious attachment. In fact, it may bring unaddressed issues to the surface. Feelings of insecurity engaging in nonmonogamy doesn't necessarily mean it's the wrong relational model for you, but it may require you to build up more security with yourself and your relationship.

Address the Issue

1. Revisit Actionable Tip 4, Build Your Relationship with Yourself (page 25). Monogamous or not, one person cannot meet all your needs all the time, so it's important to build your own community, your own interests, and so on. This will help you feel more secure. Intentionally plan things for yourself when your partner is out with other people.

2. Next, offer yourself self-validation (Tool 2, page 34). Jealousy is often judged, but it's just a feeling, much like sadness or happiness. Be kind to yourself. You can tell yourself, *It's normal to feel insecure when my partner is out meeting new people. Meeting new partners doesn't mean I'm going to be abandoned.*

3. Build self-trust by answering the questions in Tool 16, Deepen Your Self-Trust (page 80), and remind yourself about how you've gotten through hard times. Also remind yourself that feelings aren't forever.

Discussion Notes: Ethical nonmonogamy is aboveboard, consensual nonmonogamy with boundaries. There are many ways to be nonmonogamous, so it's important to communicate what you're looking for. Before diving in, have conversations about boundaries and expectations. Read books about it together, and come to agreements that meet both of your needs. It's critical for both parties to be willing to renegotiate and check in with each other frequently. Nonmonogamy takes more work and communication than other relational styles, but it can be very rewarding. It's also OK to realize you're monogamous.

Don't force yourself into something inauthentic to keep a relationship. Stay true to yourself, always.

Situation 14: Long-Distance Love

Ashleigh and her boyfriend, DeVon, are living separately while Ashleigh's out of state completing her PhD. They've been dating for four years and have talked about getting married after she graduates. Recently, Ashleigh's been feeling insecure. DeVon seems more distant—he doesn't call or text as often, and he's quieter than usual on the phone. On his last visit, he seemed less affectionate. Ashleigh needs to focus on school, but she finds herself ruminating about the relationship during class and homework. One night, when DeVon was too tired to call, she had an anxiety attack and couldn't stop crying. She worries, *Is he still committed to me?*

What's Really Going On?

DeVon isn't feeling distant because he's uncommitted; he's sad and missing Ashleigh, but he doesn't want to distract her from school. Similarly, Ashleigh doesn't want to burden DeVon with her anxiety, but she's suffering alone, which creates resentment. Long-distance relationships are especially hard for the anxiously attached. Without regular contact from their partner, the anxious person's emotions escalate. For couples in a long-distance relationship, the minimum I recommend is texting in the morning, afternoon, and evening, plus a phone call at least once a day. Regular checkpoints throughout the day help the anxious partner feel prioritized. At the same time, it's good self-regulation to avoid telling yourself made-up stories about what the other person is thinking. If you don't know, ask!

Address the Issue

1. Remember Actionable Tip 3, Take the Lead (page 24). If you need to express a concern to your partner, do it! Don't let it linger for longer than 24 hours whenever possible. Just communicate using vulnerability and not blame.

2. Don't assume what your partner is feeling—ask with curiosity instead. Curiosity (Tool 12, page 67) expresses, "I want to understand." Try this: "I'm feeling distance between us. The story I'm telling myself is you're doubting the relationship, but I want to hear what's really going on for you."

3. Is there another interpretation for why your partner is distant? What's a more generous interpretation (Tool 13, page 70) you can tell yourself instead of assuming the worst?

4. Finally, use Tool 19, Assertive Vulnerability (page 91), to ask what's going on. "I'm feeling disconnected, and I've been spiraling about it. Can you reassure me and let me know what's going on for you? That will help me feel closer to you."

Discussion Notes: Being apart from the person you love is painful! It's OK to feel sad. You'll feel better if you check in regularly and build up your community. Actionable Tip 4, Build Your Relationship with Yourself (page 25), will come in handy here. Instead of pinning all your happiness on your partner (you'll end up disappointed), focus some energy on yourself, your goals, and your community to develop a better balance for both of you.

Situation 15: Relentless Reassurance

Sam and Jade just got married after three years together. Sam has always struggled with anxiety and self-esteem issues, but recently he's feeling even more stirred up. Any time Jade looks even slightly annoyed, he immediately starts nervously asking, "Are you mad? Is everything OK?" Jade tries to be patient, but she's starting to feel overwhelmed by his persistent questioning. It doesn't matter how often she reassures Sam; he won't trust her words. Sam knows he's being insecure, but he can't stop himself from constantly checking in.

What's Really Going On?

If you can relate to Sam, perhaps someone in your earlier life (e.g., a parent, caregiver, coach) may not have been trustworthy. Maybe they *said* everything was fine, but the vibes were off. Or maybe they punished you later with passive-aggressiveness. If this was your experience, take time to learn to differentiate the past from the present. Sometimes your partner isn't upset at you; they just had a bad day! Or they're slightly irritated, but it's not a huge deal, and they'll be over it soon. Not everything is worth digging into, and discerning a real issue from something you can let go is a sign of wisdom.

Address the Issue

1. Take radical accountability (Actionable Tip 1, page 22). Everyone needs reassurance sometimes, but there's only so much others can give us. At a certain point, it's up to us to self-regulate.

2. Next, self-validate (Tool 2, page 34). You might say, *I'm just anxious. It's OK to feel scared. It's hard for me when I think someone is upset at me, but I'm not sure that's true yet.*

3. Give yourself some relief with breathing exercises (Tool 3, page 37). If your mind is ruminating, allow yourself to focus on breathing for several minutes until you feel calmer.

4. Revisit Tool 13, Find the Most Generous Interpretation (page 70). Are you 100 percent certain your partner is upset at you? Is there a more generous possibility? Perhaps they've had a bad interaction with a coworker, or maybe they have a headache. Other people's moods often don't have anything to do with us.

5. If you're still ruminating, use Tool 12, Lean on Curiosity (page 67), to check in with your partner. "I'm noticing you're quiet, and the story I'm telling myself is that you're upset at me. I know that may not be true, and it helps to hear what's going on for you."

Discussion Notes: If your relationship has a history of passive-aggressiveness, it's harder to let little moments go without worrying about the repercussions. However, it's up to us as individuals to communicate when we're upset. Checking in constantly is a form of hypervigilance; you're checking on the other person's mood to stay in control of the situation. It's exhausting for all! Trust that others are adults who can let you know if they're upset. It's not your job to guess or relentlessly ask.

Situation 16: Baby Makes Three

Since having a baby, Gia and Marco are fighting more frequently about housework and the mental load. Gia gets frustrated when Marco doesn't acknowledge household tasks, like dishes, bottle washing, and groceries. In her mind, she's doing so much with the newborn; can't he just take over some other chores? Why doesn't he see there's no more milk, the unwashed empty bottles, or when formula is low? She's bottling her frustration until she sees him playing *Call of Duty* and blows up: "Are you a child?! Look at the dishes in the sink! I can't be your mom, too!"

What's Really Going On?

A common reason couples come to therapy is because they're struggling after the birth of a child. Research from the Gottman Institute shows that nearly 67 percent of couples report relationship strife after having a baby. I see this dynamic between men and women especially. Mental load consists of thinking about the entire household's necessities, planning for them, making lists, and so on. This usually falls on the women. Well-intentioned men say, "Just make me a list; I'll do it!"

But that makes the woman the "manager" of the household. If you're having similar fights with your partner, find ways to stay respectful and work as a team. That means taking responsibility for the entirety of a task and not micromanaging one another.

Address the Issue

1. There's a reason Take Radical Accountability (page 22) is Actionable Tip 1. I know it's annoying when others don't acknowledge what we think is important, but we have control over only ourselves. Think about how you can be your best self, and you are more likely to inspire the same in your partner.

2. Reflect on gratitude (Tool 15, page 76). What is your partner getting right? It's impossible they're doing *everything* wrong (no matter what it seems like). Noticing what's right can put you in a more positive headspace. Use gratitude to get the change you want: "I see you taking care of the dog while I'm focused on the baby, and I appreciate it. It would be even more helpful to me if you took over ordering groceries. What do you think?"

3. Finally, use Tool 19 (page 91) to help you ask for your needs with assertive vulnerability. "I'm feeling overwhelmed by all my tasks. I sense myself wanting to blame you for not doing enough, but I know that won't help either of us. Can we sit down and divide the responsibilities? That will help me feel heard and lighten my load."

Discussion Notes: You're never in control of how someone responds. If you really can't get your partner to hear you, and you're using vulnerability and healthy communication, you may both need more time to settle into your new communication pattern. Couples therapy can generate increased understanding.

9

Breakups and Letting Go

Learning when to leave is just as important as learning to recognize a secure partner and maintain a relationship. Yet, anxiously attached folks often struggle with leaving relationships. There are many reasons people avoid breakups, but a big reason is holding off grief and the pain of abandonment. Even if you're the one leaving, feelings of abandonment come roaring to the surface. Many anxious people get stuck in the bargaining phase of grief, the "what-ifs." *What if I just loved them more, tried harder?* When your self-trust is higher, it'll be easier to know when it's time to go and take the necessary steps.

Situation 17: Functional Alcoholism

Chandra's husband has functional alcoholism, meaning he's able to maintain a job and appear outwardly free of issues. But Chandra knows the truth: He's drinking until 2 a.m. almost every night. Upon arriving home, he grabs a six-pack as he heads to his man cave, with barely a word to the family. When she brings up concerns for his health or how she's impacted, he becomes defensive or gives the silent treatment. If he's hungover, she'll lie for him to keep up appearances with the kids or extended family. She's embarrassed to admit this is her marriage.

What's Really Going On?

The media shows people getting wasted or belligerent, but there are many other presentations. Alcohol is physiologically addictive, meaning many people can't quit on their own. Overcoming alcohol addiction often needs to be under a doctor's care to avoid dangerous side effects. Alcoholism runs in Chandra's family, so this dynamic feels familiar and even normal. If you grew up in a home with addiction, caretaking, or codependence, be careful not to fall into caretaking in your relationships. While Chandra is not at fault for her husband's issues or conduct, she is enabling some behavior by not setting boundaries for herself and the family. My message to Chandra and everyone who can relate: Let people face their consequences—don't lie to protect them.

Address the Issue

1. Start with Actionable Tips 1 and 3, Take Radical Accountability (page 22) and Take the Lead (page 24). You're in control of only yourself, and no amount of convincing will change someone who's not ready. When someone is struggling with addiction and is unwilling to change, it'll require you to take the lead in the situation, even if it's unfair. That means making choices that are best for you and any children you may have, regardless of what the other person is doing.

2. Next, use Tool 19, Assertive Vulnerability (page 91), to express your feelings and prepare to set boundaries. "I can't keep lying to our family about your drinking. It's unhealthy for all of us. If you're unwilling to talk about it or get help, I may have to move out with the kids."

3. It's possible that your partner will blow back against your new boundary. Answer the questions in Tool 11, Handling Pushback (page 62), and formulate the best way to respond without overexplaining yourself. "I won't be making excuses for your hangovers anymore. You don't have to agree, but this is where I am with it."

4. Toxic guilt is a common issue that keeps people stuck in relationships where addiction is an issue. Fill out the worksheet in Understanding Guilt (Tool 10, page 59), and remind yourself why you're setting boundaries: to uphold your values.

Discussion Notes: It's never my place to tell people when to leave a relationship. That decision must be entirely yours. If you've continuously communicated vulnerably and set healthy boundaries, but there's no change, it may be time to reevaluate whether this relationship is viable. Staying "for the kids" is not usually a good idea. It can make children feel responsible, and it's important to take accountability for your own personal reasons for staying, like feeling guilty or preventing grief. As painful as it is, sometimes leaving is the final push that forces someone with an addiction to get sober.

Situation 18: Moving On

Liam and his college sweetheart broke up after two years together. While he feels it was the right decision, Liam is having a hard time moving on. They've been broken up for almost six months, but late at night, he finds himself scrolling her social media. Part of him finds comfort in seeing updates on her life, but another part is insecurely hanging on. One night, he sees a new post with a young man he doesn't recognize. *Has she started dating someone new?* Now Liam's mind is spiraling and he can't sleep. He's tempted to message her asking if she's moved on.

What's Really Going On?

It makes sense to be interested in an old flame's life. You cared about them once, and it's hard to shut off those feelings entirely. However, it can be wise to break contact—including looking at each other's social media—for an agreed amount of time. This will give you the space you need to actually move on. From a more detached place, you might be able to maintain a friendship or at least feel happy for them when you see their life updates. If their social media feed brings you anxiety, cut yourself off for your own self-preservation.

Address the Issue

1. Looking up your ex is understandable, but you're hurting your own feelings. Only you can stop! Start by circling back to reliable Actionable Tip 1, Take Radical Accountability (page 22). How can you use this tip to help you?

2. Deepen your self-trust (Tool 16, page 80) by reminding yourself of a time you've overcome something painful. It could be another breakup, loss, or anything that brought you emotional discomfort. *What helped me recover? What did I learn?*

3. Next, reframe your expectations (Tool 9, page 56). Are you being reasonable with yourself? Maybe you need more time to get over your ex. Constantly seeing updates on their life is keeping you stuck in the past. Give yourself some space and grace.

4. Finish up with Tool 2, Self-Validation (page 34). Your feelings make sense. Be kind to yourself. *I'm sad and still missing my ex. Looking them up is a way to stay connected. It's OK if I'm still feeling lonely and grieving the breakup.*

Discussion Notes: Everyone moves at their own speed, but most people need a minimum of several months with no contact to get over an ex. Do whatever it takes. Mute or block them on social media. Agree not to contact each other, and if one of you does, set a boundary: "I need more time to move on before we speak. It's not personal, and I hope you are well." Remember, it's up to *you* to uphold your own boundaries. This is how you build self-trust, and that will lead to more security.

Situation 19: Longing for More

Rashmi and Nick have been dating for a few years, and Rashmi is ready for children. Nick is unsure about kids, as he's told her many times. Every time they talk about it, Rashmi seems convinced he'll change his mind. She pushes for them to set a timeline and start trying, and she gets mad when Nick wants to hold off. Nick is similarly frustrated, wondering, *Why isn't she listening to my concerns?* They get into awful fights about it, where they both end up feeling exhausted, angry, and hopeless.

What's Really Going On?

Couples often ask me, "Are we incompatible?" The answer is usually no—most conflict is based on misunderstanding and negative communication cycles that can be improved. There are a few exceptions. You can't have half a baby. You're either in agreement about having one or not. If your partner doesn't want children and you do, *you* must search your heart to figure out if you're willing to sacrifice a family to stay in the relationship. Be very careful. If there's any chance you'll resent or punish the other person for "making you" sacrifice your dream of a family, you shouldn't stay. Don't avoid the grief of a breakup and accidentally replace it with the grief of regret.

Address the Issue

1. All roads lead to Actionable Tip 1, Take Radical Accountability (page 22). We have to take accountability for what we want. We can't blame the other person—it's our job to be aware of our needs and hold our boundaries.

2. If your partner doesn't want children, you cannot convince them with the best counterarguments in the world. Look at Tool 8, Respecting Others' Boundaries (page 53). Just like you want to be heard, the same respect must be given to your partner. You can explore your deeper meanings around children, but you may never come to a satisfying agreement. "I hear that you're unsure if you want children at all. Tell me more about your reservations and what having a family means to you."

3. Use self-validation (Tool 2, page 34) to honor your own feelings. *I want a family. I'm sad and hurt that my partner and I aren't on the same page. This is hard. I'm avoiding grief.*

4. Finally, spend time reflecting on Tool 6, Boundaries Versus Requests (page 47). Having children is a boundary worth holding onto if it's something you want in your life. Sometimes that might mean leaving a relationship in which the other person is unable to give you what you need. "I'm certain I want children at this point. If you're still

unsure, we're not a long-term match, and we need to talk about that."

Discussion Notes: Sadly, love isn't enough by itself to keep a relationship together. Shared values and life goals are needed for couples to align in the long term. Serious misalignments in either of those categories will cause unmanageable relationship conflict. It's unfair to you and to your partner to stay together if your needs can't be met, especially if you're resentful. Choose temporary grief over a lifetime of resentment. Grief fades, but resentment can last forever.

Situation 20: Difficult People

Ivana's husband, Charlie, has anger management issues. When Ivana accidentally dropped his phone and broke the screen, he assumed she did it purposely and barraged her with insults. Attempts to repair turn into Ivana groveling for Charlie's forgiveness because he solely blames her—*she's* the problem! He can't take accountability for his part. Ivana tries to validate his feelings, requesting couples therapy. He refuses, saying, "I'm not gonna pay someone to tell me I'm the bad guy for an hour!" Charlie doesn't give Ivana any generous interpretation, even as she desperately tries to understand him. She tells herself he's traumatized, and if she's just more patient and empathetic, he'll soften. No, Ivana—this is emotional abuse.

What's Really Going On?

Both Charlie and Ivana grew up in abusive homes. It's hard to grow up in an environment with yelling and belittlement, but it's easy to re-create it as an adult. Welcome to relational trauma. As a card-carrying member, I can tell you that one hallmark of surviving abuse is trying repeatedly to get difficult people to love you. Secure people recognize they don't deserve to be treated this way and leave sooner. Insecure, traumatized people try to convince someone to treat them with respect. In cases like this, it never works.

Address the Issue

1. Take radical accountability (Actionable Tip 1, page 22). Your part is that you keep trying to open a locked door. It's locked, and only the other person has the key. If they're unwilling to unlock it, you're frustrating both of you by continuing to knock.

2. If your partner can't (or won't) hear you, it's time to set a boundary. Tool 6, Boundaries Versus Requests (page 47), can help. "I understand your fears about therapy. No one wants to be the bad guy. I can't stay in a relationship with this much hostility and anger. If you're unwilling to work on this through therapy, I have to take care of myself by leaving."

3. If your partner has anger issues, you can expect pushback if you try to leave. Prepare for this with Tool 11, Handling Pushback (page 62). Keep your explanation simple, and have an exit plan (see box on the next page).

Discussion Notes: Emotionally abusive people may threaten to harm you, themselves, or a pet if you leave. They may become mean and angry. This is manipulation, and it comes from their pain and low self-worth. You can empathize with their pain while still setting boundaries. You deserve better, and they need to go on their own healing journey with a professional to understand why they use control to make people stay. Leaving is also the beginning of *your* self-love journey.

> Abuse Is Never OK
> ## How to Get Help
> Learning new relationship skills and how to set boundaries is helpful, but even the most useful tools rarely work when there's domestic violence or in emotionally abusive situations. Abuse is characterized by belittlement, manipulation, and control. If you're worried you're experiencing abuse, seeking professional help is a good first step. You can start by calling the National Domestic Violence Hotline at 800-799-SAFE (7233).
>
> You don't have to do this alone, and creating a safety plan with someone supportive will make it easier to leave. You deserve to feel safe and respected.

Situation 21: Filling the Void

Being single can be hard for the anxiously attached. Victor has been a serial monogamist for years. He loves being in love—it's so exciting! Because he moves quickly in relationships, he ends up disappointed when a new partner isn't who he expected after a few months. When the relationship ends, he's vigorously swiping right on dating apps within the week. Victor's not allowing himself to fully grieve, and he's not in touch with his deeper relationship needs. He's basing connection purely on "vibes" and not on shared values and goals.

What's Really Going On?

Committing and moving on too quickly are both traits of anxious attachment. Being single for a few months is usually a mature choice post-breakup. It gives you a chance to examine what happened in your last relationship, what part you played, and how you may want to behave differently going forward. If you don't take time to reflect, you'll keep repeating the same patterns. Getting attached purely on attraction is also unwise. For a relationship to be sustainable over the long term requires shared values, goals, and dreams for the future.

Address the Issue

1. Start with Actionable Tip 4, Build Your Relationship with Yourself (page 25). To be in healthy relationships with others, you need to know yourself. Take some time to explore

your own life and interests separate from a romantic partner.

2. Identify your needs (Tool 7, page 50). What do you need in your relationships? What are your values? What do you imagine for your future? Once you know these answers, it'll be easier to find someone who's aligned.

3. Deepen your self-trust (Tool 16, page 80). Is it hard for you to be alone? Remind yourself that you'll get through it by filling out the questions on this tool's worksheet. Even breakups can be excellent learning opportunities.

4. Finally, use Tool 15, Gratitude (page 76). Try to find the things in your life that you're grateful for. What's going well? Build on that, and the right person can be a lovely addition instead of the entire purpose of your life.

Discussion Notes: There's nothing wrong with enjoying partnership. Many people find fulfillment from relationships, and it's human to want connection with others. A problem arises, however, when we cannot be alone—we may unconsciously use others to fill a void within us, and that's not authentic connection. If you want to genuinely connect with others, you must know your needs and balance them with the needs of the relationship. This is how you maintain that perfect balance of me, you, and us.

Situation 22: Family Dynamics

Noah's sister struggles with addiction, and his wife, Lynn, worries that their boundaries are unhealthy. She understands Noah wants to be a good brother, but his sister frequently calls at 3 a.m., drunk and demanding a ride. She shows up at their house intoxicated, causing a scene in front of their children. When Lynn gets upset, Noah gets angry and takes his sister's side. His whole family tells Lynn, "She's his sister, you have to understand!" Lynn feels trapped. On one hand, she desperately wants to set boundaries. On the other, she knows family is important to Noah.

What's Really Going On?

"Family" has different meanings to different people and cultures. That said, this is *triangulation*, in which two people cannot directly confront their own tensions, so they fight about a third party. There are multiple triangles at play here: Noah can't confront his sister, so he and Lynn fight over what boundaries to set. Lynn and Noah can't be direct either, so they fight about his sister. Round and round it goes! The best way to stop triangulation is by talking openly about the deeper issue (not the third party) or by removing yourself altogether. Communication is best in straight lines, not triangles.

Address the Issue

1. Take radical accountability (Actionable Tip 1, page 22). What's your side of the triangle? What can you do differently?

2. Use assertive vulnerability (Tool 19, page 91) to directly communicate the deeper meaning. Instead of fighting about the third party, say, "This is about more than your sister. This is about feeling like our family's well-being is unprioritized. I need to talk about that."

3. Circle back to Tool 6, Boundaries Versus Requests (page 47). You'll recall that boundaries are about what *you're* going to do. They require others to do nothing different. Don't ask others to change. Instead, try, "If your sister comes around drunk again, I'm going to call the psychiatric emergency team. This is for the safety of our children."

4. Finally, try Tool 22, Write It Out (page 102). Sometimes we need time to express ourselves skillfully and vulnerably. Write the angry, impulsive version of what you need to say, then edit using the communication tools: "I see how unfair my boundaries feel when you're trying to be a good brother. At the same time, I'm scared of how the relationship with your sister is impacting us and our children. I need my fears to be heard, too. If you can't set boundaries with your sister, I'll have to set my own boundaries with you."

Discussion Notes: Anxiously attached people may struggle to set or maintain boundaries, and there's no perfect solution. It's especially challenging when it seems like the issue is a third party and not your partner. However, keep in mind that the third party wouldn't be an issue if your partner weren't also enabling them. You can't force anyone to set boundaries, but you can set your own. Ultimately, you have to make sure you are safe. Sometimes that means removing yourself and children from unsafe situations.

Situation 23: Undiagnosed

In the past year, Akira has noticed her husband, Max, has periods when he becomes obsessed with something new. A few months ago, it was Bitcoin, and Akira had to stop him from investing all their savings. Then, he suddenly quit his job, bought expensive professional film equipment, and became a full-time influencer. He doesn't have experience shooting or editing videos, but he's up all night trying to figure it out. His mood is strange and irritable. He's more forgetful than ever and loses track of time and appointments. When Akira asked how he plans to pay the rent this month, he flew off the handle. He's unpredictable and it's starting to scare her.

What's Really Going On?

Recognizing symptoms of mental illness is tricky without training. If your partner is suddenly acting differently, pay attention. What I've just described could be symptoms of mania, a serious recurring mental health condition that requires medication. There is much stigma around mental health, but mental health *is* physical health. Your brain is an organ, just like your pancreas. If you needed insulin, would you judge yourself? Still, it's not uncommon for people with mental illness to deny treatment altogether, largely due to stigma. It can be incredibly difficult to be in relationship with someone with an undiagnosed and untreated mental illness. Similar to addiction, you cannot force someone to get help. You can only express your feelings and set boundaries. The rest is up to the other person.

Address the Issue

1. This is very hard, but take radical accountability (Actionable Tip 1, page 22). You cannot force someone to get treatment. Adults have autonomy. You can be responsible only for yourself.

2. Circle back to Tool 9, Reasonable Expectations (page 56), and explore if your expectations need to be readjusted. If they're having a mental health crisis, they're not in their right mind. You may have to focus on your own decisions.

3. Use assertive vulnerability (Tool 19, page 91) to express concern with care. "I love you, and I'm worried about the changes I've seen in your behavior recently. I need you to get professionally evaluated."

4. Enlist Tool 6, Boundaries Versus Requests (page 47). If someone can't make good choices for themselves, you'll have to make the best choice for you. "I'm scared of what's happening. I can't stay in a relationship with this much instability if you won't get help."

Discussion Notes: Many people associate codependence with addiction, but it applies to mental illness, too. Anxious people often enable their partner's behavior by protecting them from consequences and not setting boundaries. Mental illness is never an excuse for abuse. Some people with mental illness need accommodations; that's fair. However, being someone's punching bag will never help someone manage their mental state. While this is hard when you love someone deeply, sometimes it's necessary to remember that love does not conquer all. You will never feel secure with someone with untreated mental instability, no matter what.

Situation 24: No-Show

Maggie and Lila have been together for two years. One night last week, Lila drove Maggie to the emergency room for acute pain, which turned out to be appendicitis. Surgery was scheduled for the next morning, so Maggie spent the night in the hospital. Lila agreed to come during visiting hours before the operation, but she didn't show. Maggie called repeatedly, but Lila never picked up. Maggie went into surgery alone. When she woke up, Lila was in her recovery room with flowers and tearful apologies. But she didn't have a good excuse for her absence. She muttered something about "work deadlines" and tried to change the subject. Maggie is hurt and angry. This isn't the first time she's felt abandoned during her time of need.

What's Really Going On?

As a child, Maggie's dad kept her separated from her terminally ill mother in a misguided attempt to protect her well-being. Sadly, her mother passed away alone in her hospital room. So, despite feeling upset by Lila's absence, Maggie is familiar with this dynamic. She's used to people checking out when they're overwhelmed by grief or fear, but she doesn't want to accept that anymore. Likewise, if you grew up in a home where people didn't show up for each other due to their own blocks, it may be challenging to hold boundaries around your self-worth. If someone isn't showing up for you, start showing up for yourself. You deserve it.

Address the Issue

1. Actionable Tip 4, Build Your Relationship with Yourself (page 25), applies here. Indeed, you deserve a relationship with someone reliable. Hold your own self-worth—no one else can do it for you.

2. Identify your needs (Tool 7, page 50). What do you need to feel safe and loved? Share your needs, and see how it unfolds: "To feel loved, I need to feel prioritized and like I can rely on you when I'm unwell. If you can't provide that, this relationship doesn't work for me."

3. Write it out (Tool 22, page 102). Sometimes our feelings are best expressed through writing. If you're upset, get it out on paper. Then, share vulnerably. Remember not to send your edited vulnerable letter via email or text, but read it in person: "I'm still feeling hurt and abandoned by what happened

in the hospital. I need us to keep promises and show up for each other. I understand you had work deadlines and felt overwhelmed by the situation. I feel for you, but I also need to respect myself. If you're unable to take accountability for this situation, I have to leave."

Discussion Notes: Choosing to leave a relationship is never easy, and it's not a decision to make lightly. More than anything, you deserve to be respected. If your partner's decisions disrespect you and your relationship, choose to respect yourself. Sometimes that means leaving. Know that leaving intentionally (not reactively) can be a powerful way to move toward security.

Conclusion

The most common feedback I hear about attachment work is that "it takes too long!" Moving from anxious to secure is a process, and sometimes it's lifelong. No person or relationship will ever be perfectly secure. Try finding the balance of "good enough."

For the record, feeling securely good enough isn't about settling for unfulfilling relationships. It's about being patient, kind, and flexible with yourself and your partner. Perfection is rigid, and rigid things break easily. Finding a good-enough balance means understanding that even secure relationships have difficult and disappointing moments. When you're more secure, hard moments don't break you, and relationships are satisfying *most* of the time.

People also commonly say, "No one speaks like this in real life. It's too cheesy!" or "I've tried talking like this, and my partners don't respond well." Cheese is delicious! Embrace the cheese. Still, tasty as it is, I never want you to use language that feels inauthentic. Feel free to change the wording to fit your vibe, but keep the spirit of vulnerability alive. As for your partner not responding well, remember that you can use a tool perfectly and the other person may react poorly. Part of security is letting go of control. It takes repeated experiences of new communication for a healthier pattern to stick. Don't give up after a few tries. Keep practicing!

Trust that security is possible, and it starts within you. Let that give you hope as you continue on your journey to feeling finally secure.

Resources

Online Resources

Bhumi Therapy Center: The author's own mindfulness-based therapy center for California residents
bhumitherapycenter.com

The Gottman Institute: A research-based approach to relationships
gottman.com

Jimmy Knowles: Relationship educator
jimmyonrelationships.com

A Little Nudge: Online dating coach
alittlenudge.com

The Secure Relationship: Expert relationship help
thesecurerelationship.com

Books

Attachment Theory in Practice by Susan M. Johnson

Break Up on Purpose by John Kim

Good Inside by Becky Kennedy

Hold Me Tight by Dr. Sue Johnson

How to Be Dateable by Julie Krafchick and Yue Xu

Opening Up: A Guide to Creating and Sustaining Open Relationships by Tristan Taormino

Polysecure: Attachment, Trauma and Consensual Nonmonogamy by Jessica Fern

Raising Securely Attached Kids by Eli Harwood

Secure Love by Julie Menanno

The Seven Principles for Making Marriage Work by John M. Gottman and Nan Silver

References

Ainsworth, Mary D. S., Mary C. Blehar, Everett Waters, and Sally Wall. *Patterns of Attachment: A Psychological Study of the Strange Situation*. Lawrence Erlbaum, 1978.

Bowlby, J. "Attachment Theory and Its Therapeutic Implications." *Adolescent Psychiatry*, no. 6 (1978), 5–33.

Bowlby, John. *A Secure Base: Parent-Child Attachment and Healthy Human Development*. Routledge, 1988.

Fern, Jessica. *Polysecure: Attachment, Trauma and Consensual Nonmonogamy*. Thorntree Press, 2020.

Gottman, John, and Nan Silver. *The Seven Principles for Making Marriage Work*. Seven Dials, 2018.

Gottman, John Mordechai, and Robert Wayne Levenson. "How Stable Is Marital Interaction over Time?" *Family Process*, vol. 38, no. 2 (June 1999): 159–65, https://doi.org/10.1111/j.1545-5300.1999.00159.x.

Harwood, Eli. *Raising Securely Attached Kids*. Sasquatch Books, 2024.

Johnson, Sue. *Hold Me Tight*. Little Brown, 2014.

Johnson, Susan M. *Attachment Theory in Practice: Emotionally Focused Therapy (EFT) with Individuals, Couples, and Families*. Guilford Press, 2019.

Kennedy, Becky. *Good Inside*. HarperCollins, 2022.

Menanno, Julie. *Secure Love*. Simon and Schuster, 2024.

Taormino, Tristan. *Opening Up: A Guide to Creating and Sustaining Open Relationships*. Cleis Press, 2007.

Index

A

abandonment, 13, 19, 53, 143
    fear of, 16, 64, 128, 132, 135
abuse, 94, 101, 150, 152, 159
accountability. *See* radical accountability
addiction, 111–13, 117, 144–46, 155, 158–59
aggression, 65, 91–93, 133
    passive, 87, 138, 139
alcoholism, 144
anger, 13, 31, 74, 107, 126, 148
    angry pursuer, 132–33
    communicating, 156
    emotional abuse and, 150–52
    sensory soothing and, 40
anxiety, 11, 13, 16–18, 23, 26, 44
    breathing exercises and, 37–39
    expression of, 96, 98
    texting, 115–16
anxious attachment, 6, 7, 10–17, 22–23, 132, 134, 153
    body signals of, 95
    boundaries for, 46, 156
    breathing exercises for, 37
    co-regulation and, 30, 102, 133
    dating with, 106, 136, 153
    leaving relationships and, 143
    people-pleasers, 50, 91

reparenting and, 20
self-validation and, 34
trust and, 66
assertive vulnerability, 51, 110, 128, 137, 156, 158
    to communicate needs, 114, 116, 141
    set boundaries with, 114, 122, 145
    as tool, 91–94
attachment styles, 10–17
attachment theory, 11
attunement, 19–20, 102
avoidant attachment, 11, 13–15, 17, 22, 54, 94
awareness, 8–9, 15, 71
    of attachment style, 10
    of body signals, 31, 62
    boundaries and, 47, 149

B

babies, 16, 23, 140–41, 148
    See also children
behavioral activation, 43
blame, 11, 22, 48, 86, 93, 98
    communicating without, 20–21, 48, 116, 137, 141, 149
    cycle of, 17, 92
body language, 19, 88, 95

body signals, 31–32, 53–55,
    95–96, 108, 132
  noticing, 35, 41, 43, 62, 64, 71
boundaries, 11, 16, 46, 117,
    144, 152
  with assertive vulnerability,
    112, 114, 122, 145, 146
  to build self-trust, 80, 83, 148
  communicating, 114
  in family dynamics, 155
  feeling painful, 112
  handling pushback, 62–65, 145
  healthy, 25, 146
  to hold self-worth, 118–19, 160
  in hookup culture, 109
  identifying and expressing
    your needs, 50–52
  maintaining, 156–57
  mental illness and, 158–59
  in nonmonogamy, 134–35
  to preserve relationships,
    112–13
  reasonable expectations,
    56–58
  versus requests, 47–49, 118,
    149, 151, 156, 158
  respecting others', 53–55,
    130, 149
  understanding guilt, 59–61, 145
  validate while setting, 101
  without blame, 93
breakups, 14, 80, 112, 118,
    146–49, 154

breathing exercises, 37–39, 108,
    128, 139
  after writing out feelings, 103
  in self-soothing, 41–42, 55, 132

C

checking in, 21, 24, 135, 137–38,
    139–40
childhood, 17, 19–20, 23, 32, 70
  anxious attachment forming
    in, 10, 15–16, 29
  attachment needs and, 50, 52
children, 6, 16, 23, 122, 129, 160
  alcoholism and, 144–45
  feeling responsible, 16, 146
  having, 148–49
  needing co-regulation, 30, 102
  safety of, 145, 155–57
  validating emotions of, 19
codependency, 111, 144, 159
communication, 17, 22, 79, 125,
    127, 163
  assertive, 133
  with assertive vulnerability,
    91, 110, 116, 156
  of boundaries, 47, 114
  with curiosity, 67–69
  of needs, 50–51, 114
  negative styles of, 85–88, 114,
    133, 148
  in relationships, 134–35, 137,
    139, 142, 146
  secure people and, 12, 20–21,
    135

taking the lead in, 25, 126
triangulation and, 155
with vulnerability, 21, 25, 48, 84, 125, 137
writing it out, 102–3, 156
conflict, 51, 57, 74, 122, 131, 150
avoiding, 11, 14
communication and, 103
curiosity and, 67, 69
expectations of, 58
insecurity in times of, 12
as misinterpretation, 70, 148
negative communication styles during, 85, 133
obsessing over, 13
radical accountability and, 89–90, 126
recurring, 126
triggers of, 32
in validation, 99
connection, 32, 50, 56, 71, 73–75, 147, 153
anxious attachment and, 13, 16
desiring, 11, 16, 53
dis-, 129, 130–32, 137
in relationships, 109–10, 115–17, 121, 130–32, 134, 153–54
safety and giving, 54
taking ownership and, 90
using vulnerability, 84, 115
contempt, 85, 87, 125
coping skills, 12, 30
breathing exercises, 37–39
move your body, 43–45
self-validation, 34–36
sensory soothing, 40–42
trigger map, 31–33
See also self-regulation
co-regulation, 30, 102, 133
criticism, 13, 17, 25, 92
as negative communication style, 85–86, 97, 98, 125, 133
taking ownership, 25, 89–90, 103, 126
curiosity, 63, 71, 88, 114, 137
to build trust, 67–69, 71, 122, 130, 139

D

dating, 10, 106–23, 134, 136, 146, 153–54
and ready for children, 148
respecting boundaries in, 53–54
self-validation and, 34–35
sensory soothing and, 40
struggling with, 7
tools to handle, 29, 105
Davis, Yeshiva, 80
defensiveness, 14, 24, 96, 101, 125, 144
assumptions and, 67
in communication style, 84, 85–86, 98
gaslighting or, 127
negative cycle of, 17

defensiveness (*continued*)
    non-, 100
    vulnerability and, 92
disappointment, 12, 35, 54, 92, 125
    in relationships, 107, 118, 120, 138, 153, 163
disorganized attachment, 14–15

E

embodiment, 95–98, 133
emotional abandonment, 13, 19, 53
emotional bank account, 73–75, 131
emotional safety, 24, 50–52, 71
emotions, 6, 11, 16, 80, 117, 124–25
    assertive vulnerability and, 91
    blame for, 17
    body signals and, 31–32
    exercise and, 43, 45
    expectations of, 57
    healthy, 133
    honesty in, 84
    internalized, 14
    in relationships, 130–31, 136
    responsibility for, 61
    self-regulation and, 20, 30, 132
    self-trust and, 147
    sensory soothing of strong, 40, 42
    triggers of, 31
    validating, 19, 35, 99

exercises
    breathing, 37–39, 41–42, 55, 103, 108, 128, 132, 139
    physical, 43–45, 103
    self-soothing, 40–42
expectations, 56–58, 122, 133, 147, 158
    for boundaries, 48, 64, 135
    in dating, 107–8, 111, 115, 117–18, 120
expressions, 21, 47, 110, 121, 131, 137
    of curiosity, 68, 137
    versus embodiment, 95–98, 133
    facial, 19, 95
    of feelings, 20, 95–96, 132–33, 145, 158
    of gratitude, 88
    of insecurity, 11
    internal, 14
    of needs, 50–51
    self-, 32, 125
    written, 103, 156, 160

F

feelings. *See* emotions
Frankl, Viktor, 8
frustration, 7, 50, 113, 126, 148, 151
    communication and, 125, 127
    expectations and, 56
    holding plank pose when feeling, 44

at mental load, 140
respecting boundaries and, 54
self-regulation and, 103
tolerating, 12
urgency and, 23

G

gaslighting, 127
generosity, 66, 75, 76–77, 121, 125
generous interpretation, 70–72, 116, 126, 137, 139
    for anger, 74
    in validation, 100
Gottman, John, 85, 126
Gottman Institute, 73, 85, 140
gratitude, 76–79, 88
grief, 143, 146, 147, 149–50, 153, 160
guilt, 19, 22, 99, 101, 132, 134
    understanding, 59–61, 112, 145–46

H

honesty, 56, 84, 110, 115, 125, 127
    boundaries and, 60, 62, 65
    in communication, 22, 69, 91
    as value, 60, 114
hookup culture, 109, 115

K

kindness, 15, 24, 25–26, 62, 103, 163
    to body signals, 53
    in communication, 125

as expectation, 57
respond to anger with, 74
self-validation and, 34–35, 135, 147
as shared value, 114
when calm, 126

L

Levenson, Robert, 126
long-distance relationships, 136–37

M

manipulation, 100, 127, 152
Menanno, Julie, 89
mental health, 111–12, 157–59
mental load, 140
mindfulness, 35, 37
monogamy, 110, 135, 153
motivation, 43–44, 69, 71

N

narcissism, 93, 94
needs, 7, 20, 21, 23, 141, 154
    boundaries and, 46, 48, 53, 114
    for emotional support, 117
    identifying and expressing, 50–52, 96, 112, 149, 154, 160
    nonmonogamy, 135
    overexplaining, 86
    partner meeting, 13, 15, 58, 118, 135, 153
    for reassurance, 139
    in touch with own, 59

nervous system, 31, 42, 43
Nin, Anaïs, 99
nonmonogamy, 134–35

O
obsession, 13, 54, 134, 157
open relationships, 134–35

P
parenting, 6, 15–16, 19–20, 51, 122, 138
patience, 7, 23–24, 128, 138, 150
   in dating, 106, 108, 122
   secure attachment takes, 21, 105, 163
pushback, 62, 112, 145, 151

R
radical accountability, 17, 22–23, 56, 69, 89–90, 141
   addiction and, 145
   in breakups, 147, 149, 151
   in dating, 110, 112, 118, 120
   mental illness and, 158
   self-regulation and, 132, 139
   in triangulation, 156
reassurance, 6, 13, 138–39
reliability, 16, 107, 114, 147, 160
reparenting, 20, 53
requests, 47–49, 118, 149, 151, 156, 158
respect, 125, 130–31, 141, 149, 151
   boundaries, 47–49, 53–54, 57, 60–61, 64

communicating with, 24, 57, 127, 129
   in dating, 107
   dis-, 93, 129, 161
   safety and, 152
   security and, 26
   self-, 24, 34, 60, 119, 161
responsibility, 48, 50, 65, 110, 132, 141, 158
   children feeling, 16–17, 146
   for emotional states, 30, 61, 103
   taking, 88, 141

S
safety, 11, 16, 22, 106, 110, 152
   boundaries and, 46, 51–52, 54, 63, 157
   of children, 156
   commitment and, 118
   communication and, 21, 25, 95, 103, 160
   emotional, 24, 50, 71
   insecure attachment and, 13
   radical accountability and, 90
   vulnerability and, 95, 128
savior role, 111
secure attachment, 6, 12, 84, 96, 119, 122
   boundaries for, 46–47
   building, 7, 11, 18–26
self-esteem, 12, 16, 45, 46, 138
self-regulation, 29–45, 103

self-soothing tool, 40–42, 54, 55, 108, 132–33
self-trust, 18, 45, 46, 80–83, 135
    breakups and, 143, 147–48, 154
self-validation, 39, 108, 110, 118, 135, 139
    to honor feelings, 26, 120, 147, 149
    tool for, 34–36
self-worth, 111, 119, 152, 160
sensory soothing, 40–42, 55, 108, 132
sex, 109–10, 117, 129–31
stonewalling, 85, 87
stress, 11, 12, 31, 35, 40, 129
    breathing exercises for, 37–38
    moving your body for, 43–45

T

triangulation, 155–57
triggers, 17, 20, 71, 132
    trigger map, 31–33, 108
trust, 19, 24, 66, 67–69, 73–75, 138
    anxious attachment and, 13, 17
    gratitude and, 76–79
    mis-, 16, 100
    secure attachment and, 12, 29, 163
    See also self-trust

V

validation, 16, 19–20, 99–101, 128
    external, 13, 18
    internal, 18, 26
    in relationships, 24, 26, 57, 150
    See also self-validation
values, 32, 59, 60, 112, 145, 154
    shared, 107, 109, 114, 122, 150, 153
vulnerability, 17, 89, 126, 129, 160, 163
    communicating with, 25, 48, 84, 125, 137, 146
    confusing with honesty, 84, 125
    connection requiring, 115
    expressing feelings with, 20, 95
    expressing needs through, 50–51
    reflecting emotional maturity, 21
    in relationships, 119, 133, 142
    set boundaries with, 112, 122
    translating, 102–3
    See also assertive vulnerability

Acknowledgments

First, I'd like to acknowledge my partner for being my secure base for nine years. Our relationship was the first secure attachment I've known, and this book wouldn't be possible without that experience. Thanks for being my first editor. I love you.

Next, I'd like to thank all of my clients. Thanks for trusting me to help you on your journeys. I hope this book can be another step on the healing path for you!

His Holiness the 17th Karmapa, it was a true honor to have You name Bhumi and support our mission. Thank You for the "once in a many lifetimes" opportunity to learn from You. May Your teachings continue to benefit all beings.

My professor, Dr. Karen Derris, who brought me to India to meet His Holiness the 17th Karmapa, has been instrumental in my life path. It was a privilege to be your student.

Last but not least, I'd like to thank my editors at Zeitgeist. Thanks for believing in me. It was a shock and a thrill to get this opportunity. Here's to many more!

About the Author

Maria Vogel, LMFT, has nine years of clinical practice experience. As a Gottman-trained couples therapist, Maria specializes in working with couples and individuals with relational trauma. With 15 years of mindfulness and meditation experience, Maria teaches clients concrete skills to handle hard moments. Her practice consists of many LGBTQ+ clients, neurodivergent folks, and people struggling with chronic illness.

In 2024, Maria founded Bhumi Marriage and Family Therapy Center, a group practice utilizing mindfulness-based therapy. The idea for Bhumi was born from Maria's time studying Tibetan Buddhism under His Holiness the 17th Karmapa in Sidhpur, India, in 2011. After finishing her master's degree in psychology, Maria felt compelled to combine her understanding of Western psychology with her appreciation of Buddhism. His Holiness gifted a name for the organization in 2015. Bhumi's mission is to help people from all walks of life manage stress, soothe anxiety, and build intentional lives.

When she's not seeing clients, Maria is exploring nature, cooking, and creating art with friends. Her therapy cat, Sugarplum, attends all sessions (virtually). Bhumi is located in the Bay Area and is open to new clients anywhere in California.

For more resources related to Bhumi and Maria's practice, check out bhumitherapycenter.com.

Hi there,

We hope *Finally Secure* helped you. If you have any questions or concerns about your book, or have received a damaged copy, please contact customerservice@penguinrandomhouse.com. We're here and happy to help.

Also, please consider writing a review on your favorite retailer's website to let others know what you thought of the book.

Sincerely,

The Zeitgeist Team